SO-AWV-459

# The Structural Hypothesis:
# An Evolutionary Perspective

# The Structural Hypothesis:
# An Evolutionary Perspective

by

Arnold Rothstein, M.D.

INTERNATIONAL UNIVERSITIES PRESS, INC.
New York

Copyright © 1983, Arnold Rothstein.

All rights reserved. No part of this book may be reproduced
by any means, nor translated into a machine language,
without the written permission of the publisher.

**Library of Congress Cataloging in Publication Data**

Rothstein, Arnold, 1936–
    The structural hypothesis.

    Bibliography: p.
    Includes index.
    1. Psychoanalysis.   2. Freud, Sigmund, 1856–1939.
I. Title.
BF173.R67   1983        150.19'52        83-18490
ISBN 0-8236-6175-X

Manufactured in the United States of America

*To*

*Arden*

*and to*

*Barbara, Chloe, Lisanne and Michelle*

# Contents

# Introduction

This book is written from a Freudian evolutionary perspective. Its purpose is to contribute to the development and elaboration of traditional metapsychology. A revolutionary perspective, such as that proposed by Schafer (1976) or Kohut (1977), views paradigms as relatively static constructs and proposes to divest psychoanalysis of old models and to substitute entirely new theories in their place. An evolutionary perspective strives to accommodate (in the Piagetian sense) the traditional model to novelty and new data. It views the corpus of psychoanalytic theory as organic and therefore open to the influence of new experience. From an evolutionary perspective, psychoanalytic theory is not conceived of as the product of one analyst's mind at a moment in time, as Gedo and Goldberg (1973) view the tripartite model. Rather, such a theory as the structural hypothesis is conceptualized as a model created by Freud over a period of time and formally presented to his colleagues in 1923 for their consideration. I believe Freud hoped that he and his colleagues would experience any model as an imperfect construct to be tested, modified, and improved in the clinical situation. This was his modus operandi, and I believe that it remains a viable legacy at this time in the development of psychoanalytic theory.

Freud was constantly striving to elaborate theory in response to his own clinical experience and that of others. His first theories, written in collaboration with Breuer and Fliess, stressed the influence of the environment and man's biological nature. Although his self-analysis shifted his emphasis to a more intrapsychic perspective, at first focused on the nature of the unconscious fantasy and later upon the elaboration of fantasy in conflict, the influence of the environment and biology on his evolving theories once muted was never relinquished. The revolutionary challenges of Jung and Adler, in addition to the increasing analytic experience of Freud and others, contributed to the elaboration of libido theory and resulted in its emendation with the introduction of the seminal and transitional concept of narcissistic or ego libido.

Freud, like most geniuses, was not often fully satisfied. The data of the war and of success neuroses, as well as increasing experience with depressed and masochistic patients and experiences of what he was coming to understand as the negative therapeutic reaction, led Freud to his most speculative elaboration of libido theory: destrudo, thanatos, the death instinct. Although Freud explicitly acknowledged the highly speculative nature of these constructs, they remained viable hypotheses for him until his death. Freud was capable of functioning on different levels of abstraction and at varying conceptual distances from the clinical data of the analytic situation. The structural hypothesis, in part, represents a less experience-distant derivative and alternative to the theory of the life and death instincts. The structural hypothesis emphasizes conflict that derives from an inner and interminable cauldron of powerful wishes and from the influences of the environment. Perhaps its most important construct is the superego, which Freud considered to develop from both aggressive and libidinal drive derivatives, and from the influence of heredity, endowment, and the impact of the external world.

In the sixty years since its introduction, the constructs of the structural hypothesis have been elaborated and commented upon by many colleagues. Differences of opinion have developed over such issues as the importance of preoedipal versus oedipal factors, nature versus nurture, and trauma versus interminable drive derivatives on the development of psychic structure. Such differences have often resulted in discussions that seemed to polarize these questions into either/or disagreements – discussions which sometimes have approached polemical proportions.

Freud's contributions in general and his structural hypothesis in particular have been elaborated by some to emphasize the oedipal phase of development and its drive derivatives. Hartmann's contributions and particularly his concept of ego and superego autonomy of function represent this perspective. Others like Melanie Klein and Bergler have emphasized preoedipal conflict and structural development. More recently Kohut has emphasized preoedipal developmental arrests. His perspective deemphasizes conflict and has influenced him to propose a model that facilitates an understanding of processes of the development and repair of a "bipolar" self.

In this book I will attempt to elaborate the concepts ego and superego to better accommodate data of interminable conflicts deriving from a variety of stages in the life cycle, as well as data reflecting traumatic influences on the development of the individual. Freud's energic hypothesis is deemphasized and treated predominantly as a metaphor, a metaphor often rich in its representational implications. While one might find energic aspects of Chapter 7 of *The Interpretation of Dreams* or *Beyond the Pleasure Principle* cumbersome, aspects of these works remain rich sources of clinical insight and inspiration.

The first section of this book explores the influence of ubiquitous and interminable irrational investments in scientific theories in general and in psychoanalytic paradigms in particular. It is a fundamental premise of Chapter 1 that the narcissistic investment of a theory contributes to a revolutionary process of paradigm competition and elaboration. I am sug-

gesting that this insight into process in science is a psychoanalytic contribution to the history of science. To the degree
that theories are divested of their narcissistic illusions of perfection, to the degree that creators and disciples mourn their
pursuit of these illusionary gratifications, the process of
developments in science can be more rational and evolutionary.

The second section of the book contributes to the evolution
of the structural hypothesis. Chapter 2, in emphasizing the
development of the representational world, offers a schema
for organizing data reflective of intrasystemic conflict of the
ego. Chapter 3 explores the interminable development of the
superego, especially its preoedipal roots, organization, and
functions. Chapter 4 explores the psychoanalytic concept of
trauma and its relationship to the repetition compulsion.
These considerations complement and elaborate issues raised
in Chapters 2 and 3. Chapters 5 and 6 examine the enigmatic
topics narcissism and masochism and elaborate these as contents of psychic structure. Finally, Chapter 7 focuses on the
dreamwork from an ego-psychological perspective. These
explications are employed to elucidate the controversy concerning the role and value of the manifest dream.

These efforts at evolving the structural hypothesis aim at
accommodating it to the enlarging scope of overdetermination. Waelder's (1936) seminal paper on the subject stressed a
"macroscopic" view of the ego's striving to assimilate interminable intersystemic conflict—conflict with the id, the compulsion to repeat, the superego, and the external world. This
book elaborates aspects of what is implicit in Waelder's paper,
as well as the considerable shifts of emphasis that have taken
place since his contribution. Chapter 2, "The Ego," explores
the "microscopic" intrasystemic conflicts and assimilative
struggles between competing self-representations-as-agents.
In 1930, data that I am suggesting is more felicitously organized under the rubric of the narcissistically, masochistically,

and sadistically invested self-representations-as-agents would probably have been ascribed to the id or, in greater synchrony with the perspective of this book, to the "pleasure-ego." Similarly my emphasis explores the repetition compulsion from the perspective of a problem-solving mode of the immature ego, rather than as a derivation from the lowermost part of the id, the biological bedrock of the death instinct. In that regard a contemporary perspective gives greater emphasis to the traumatic influences of the real parental object on the process of the development of psychic structure and the elaboration of character through inter- and intrasystemic conflict.

Finally, a fundamental value of an evolutionary Freudian perspective is a reemphasis of Freud's original stress on the value of insight into the interminably irrational nature of man. This perspective is advantageous both for theory elaboration and for understanding the mode of therapeutic action of psychoanalysis.

# Part I

## Toward an Evolutionary Perspective

# CHAPTER 1

# Psychoanalytic Paradigms and Their Narcissistic Investment

*Unfortunately, however, people are seldom impartial where ultimate things, the great problems of science and life are concerned. Each of us is governed in such cases by deep internal prejudices, into whose hands our speculations unwittingly play.*

Sigmund Freud, *Beyond the Pleasure Principle*

In *The Structure of Scientific Revolutions,* Kuhn describes the development of and competition between scientific paradigms and suggests that this revolutionary process is less than rational: "A decision between alternate ways of practicing . . . must be based less on past achievement than on future promise. . . . A decision of that kind can only be made on faith" (pp. 157–158). In responding to critics, Kuhn (1970) reiterates that the explication of paradigm development "must be psychological, . . . a description of a value system, an ideology" (p. 21).

This chapter explores the irrational elements in paradigm development and competition from a psychoanalytic perspective and proposes that conscious attention to these irrational investments facilitates an *evolutionary,* rather than a *revolutionary,* development of paradigms.

9

According to Kuhn (1962) the term *paradigm,* or *disciplinary matrix,* is used "in two different senses. . . . It stands for the entire constellation of beliefs, values, techniques. . . shared by members of a given community. . . . It denotes one sort of element in that constellation, the concrete puzzle-solutions which, employed as models or examples, can replace explicit rules as a basis for the solution of the remaining puzzles" (p. 175). The problem in normal science is that paradigm development, propagation, and competition reflect the nature of scientists rather than of science. "Effective research scarcely begins before a scientific community thinks it has acquired firm answers to questions like the following: What are the fundamental entities of which the universe is composed?" Furthermore, "Answers to questions like these are firmly embedded in the educational initiation that prepares and licenses the student for professional practice. Because the education is both rigorous and rigid these answers come to exert a deep hold on the scientific mind" (pp. 4–5). Students learn to "accept theories on the authority of the teacher and text, not because of evidence" (p. 80). The research of established normal science thus becomes a "strenuous and devoted attempt to force nature into the conceptual boxes supplied by professional education" (p. 5).

The result of this process is that "normal science often suppresses fundamental novelties because they are necessarily subversive to its basic commitments" (p. 5), that scientists do not "normally aim to invent new theories," and that "they are often intolerant of those invented by others" (p. 24). There are, however, conditions that lead to the proposal of new theories and a resulting competition between paradigm proponents: "When the profession can no longer evade anomalies that subvert the existing tradition, . . . then begin extraordinary investigations that lead the profession to a new set of commitments, a new basis for the practice of science." These events are "scientific revolutions, . . . tradition-shattering

tering complements to the tradition-bound activity of normal science" (p. 6). The world within which work is done is seen as transformed: "A 'visual gestalt' is changed. The marks on the paper that were first seen as a bird are now seen as an antelope" (p. 85). Such paradigm change alters "the data themselves" (p. 135), "scientists look in new places ... see new things" (p. 111).

The community is divided. The defenders of the old paradigm struggle to "devise numerous articulations and ad hoc modifications of their theory in order to eliminate any apparent conflict" (p. 78). The proponents of the new tend to seek authority for it by attributing its creation to one person: "We so readily assume that discovering, like seeing or touching, should be unequivocally attributable to an individual and at a moment in time" (p. 55).

Of course, Kuhn is writing about the so-called hard sciences – physics, chemistry, astronomy, etc. He regards psychoanalysis as a discipline at a stage in which its tools cannot isolate factors with sufficient clarity to be considered a hard science. "Contemporary psychoanalysis" is like an older nineteenth-century medicine: Its "shared theory was adequate only to establish the plausibility of the discipline and to provide a rationale for the various craft-rules which governed practice. The rules had proved their use in the past, but no practitioner supposed they were sufficient to prevent recurrent failure" (p. 8). Waelder (1960), who also regards psychoanalysis as a soft science, feels that it will always be concerned with a multifactorial field requiring a synthetic approach to the data.

Psychoanalysis is in a preparadigmatic period with regard to its ability to validate its "concrete puzzle solutions." Waelder's emphasis on overdetermination leads him to stress that psychoanalysis will of necessity generate models that deal with a multiplicity of factors to explain the compromise formations resulting from the ego's interminable assimilative efforts. Things are still more complex. Contemporary psychoanalytic models that strive to conceptualize the therapeutic actions of psychoanalysis must accommodate not only the results of the analysand's assimilative work, but, in addition, factors referrable both to the analyst's personality and to temporal considerations of process. Questions remain concerning the influence of the analyst's personality on his attraction for particular theories, the influence these theories exert upon him, and the evolving analytic relationship and process.

In spite of these views, it is worth asking what light Kuhn's concept of revolutionary process in science can shed on the development of paradigms in psychoanalysis. His work suggests a number of questions that will be explored in this chapter: (1) What irrational factors influence and contribute to the process of paradigm elaboration? (2) What factors contribute to an individual's becoming a "creator" of a paradigm? (3) What factors attract practitioners to a particular paradigm? (4) What factors contribute to the feeling in some that it is time for a new paradigm? (5) What are the modes of altering the established paradigm?

With regard to the first question, it is my premise that the narcissistic investment of a theory contributes an irrational element to paradigm evolution. The narcissistically invested theory is perceived (consciously or unconsciously) to be perfect. It is felt to be the ultimate provider of answers for its practitioner. As such, it assuages his sense of vulnerability and helplessness. Armed with the narcissistically invested paradigm, the practitioner can face the uncertainty of the clinical situation.

In his elaboration of the ego ideal and of ubiquitous defensive investments in children and religion, Freud (1914) emphasizes man's unwillingness to relinquish definitively his primary narcissistic perfection. Wilhelm Reich (1933) defines explicitly what Freud has implied, "that the character is essentially a narcissistic protection mechanism" (p. 158). With the decline of religion as a viable repository for narcissistic investment, man has increasingly turned to other institutions to serve as the idealized objects for his illusions of perfection. At the same time, he has exhibited resistance to exploring these narcissistic investments: "We dislike being shown to be at the mercy of unconscious religious, political, ethnic patterns. . . [shown] the dependence on social structures of our physical and emotional existence and well-being" (Erikson, 1954, p. 39).

Kuhn (1962) describes the scientist as "concerned to understand the world and to extend the precision and scope with which it has been ordered" (p. 42). The scientist subliminally perceives his helplessness. Intellect is invested as the vehicle actively to undo that helplessness. He seeks to defend against accepting his intellectual limitations by adopting the narcissistically invested theory that holds out the possibility of having all the answers. He internalizes a representation of the narcissistically invested theory into his self-representation: he is a Freudian, a Kleinian, a Jungian, a Sullivanian, or, now, a Kohutian, and as such he is armed to feel he has the answer.

Freud's position was somewhat different from our own. He was a lonely, ambitious pioneer without a psychoanalytic paradigm to invest narcissistically. He gained sustenance instead from friendships with idealized colleagues like Breuer and Fliess, and he narcissistically invested the theories of the physical sciences of his day. He struggled to transpose these illusions of perfection onto the theories of the new field he was helping to create. In 1895, Freud stated: "The intention of this project is to furnish us with a psychology which shall be a *natural science:* its aim, that is, is to represent psychical processes as . . . *void of contradiction*" (p. 355, emphasis added). Throughout his life whenever Freud was faced with the limits of his theory, with its imperfections, he relied on biological solutions, a practice drawn from his belief that a discernible answer existed in the natural sciences. If the mind were built on a physical substrate of neurons mediating tangible forces of energy (Q) characterized by measurable resistances at contact barriers, Freud believed answers would be found. In 1900 he stated: "The explanation no doubt lies in relations of energy of which we have no knowledge" (p. 577). Metaphors such as the "death instinct" (1923a, p. 40), "constitutional bisexuality" (1923a, p. 33), "adhesiveness of the libido" (1916a, p. 348), and "psychical inertia" (1937, pp. 241–242) were coined to explain what Freud could not explain with constructs that were closer to emotional experience. Theoretical explanations steeped in biology are narcissistically invested and help an analyst live more comfortably with the limits of his psychological understanding. In such a manner, Freud believed the limited therapeutic efficacy of analysis, its interminability, to be rooted in the "bedrock" of "the biological field" (p. 252).

Kuhn's argument (1962) points toward the second and third questions raised above: What factors select a creator and attract his followers? "How an individual invests (or finds he has invented) a new way of giving order to data. . . must here remain inscrutable and may be permanently so. Let us here note only one thing about it. Almost always the men who achieve these fundamental inventions. . . have been either very young or very new to the field" (p. 90). They are "men so young . . . that practice has committed them less deeply than most of their contemporaries to the world view and rules of the old paradigm" (p. 144). We would elaborate this by saying that their narcissistic investment in the established paradigm is not yet so rigidly integrated. Their egos may integrate their narcissism in a defiant manner (Freud, 1917b), providing them with what Erikson (1954) terms "divine mistrust" (p. 37). In addition, the void created by the increasing awareness of the limits of the existing paradigm attracts a young practitioner who can see himself as a creator of a new paradigm. The creator has an internalized sense of what Ferenczi (1913) calls the "omnipotence of thoughts." For an individual to have the feeling that he can create a new paradigm, his thinking as an aspect of self-representation has to be narcissistically invested. This investment is usually unconscious. At the inspirational moment, the creator feels himself to be omniscient. These feelings interact with his talent and with serendipitous events in his discipline to allow him to create a new synthesis, a new paradigm.

Among the many factors of Freud's development that influenced the forging of his personality and the narcissistic investment of his thinking, two deserve emphasis. He was a first-born, adulated male child, which contributed to the maintenance and intensity of his deeply felt sense of perfection. The death of a sibling at the height of his rapprochement subphase very probably reinforced his sense of the omnipotence of his wishes and thoughts. The rest is history.

Growing awareness of the limits of an established paradigm results in "a period of pronounced professional insecurity" (Kuhn, 1962, p. 67). Some paradigm practitioners restlessly struggle to explain the defects of the established paradigm, while others pursue new illusions of perfection. Thus, dissatisfaction with the explanatory power of psychoanalytic theory has led a number of psychoanalysts – such as George Klein (1976), Peterfreund (1971), Schafer (1976), and Kohut (1977) – to propose new paradigms. It is interesting to note that these analysts are mature, successful, and well established as respected colleagues in the psychoanalytic community, in contrast to the typically younger creator of the hard sciences. This fact may be significantly influenced by the "educational initiation" (Kuhn, 1962, p. 5) that is characteristic of the psychoanalyst's experience. Lichtenberg (1978) in elaborating this point suggests that the power of the transference as a component of an analyst's personal psychoanalysis is an aspect of the initiation that further accentuates the irrational polemical aspects of paradigm competition. The general tendency of scientists to idealize paradigms is encouraged within every analyst's clinical psychoanalysis. Lichtenberg reminds us that the splits and cleavages that have occurred throughout the history of psychoanalysis have often followed lines based on allegiance to or rebellion against a dominant local analyst who has been both administrative leader or personal analyst to many of the next generation.

Most analysts enter an institute at an age when their successful contemporaries in physics have already completed work that may prove revolutionary for that discipline. I have proposed that the potential creator has a personality organization characterized by a repetitive effort to restore a sense of narcissistic perfection to his self-representation. As a young person, the future analytic creator finds himself facing a life cycle replete with way stations typified by well-defined, narcissistically invested goals. He seeks admission to a good college, medical school, internship, residency, and institute.[1] He works to become a graduate analyst only to find himself, at midlife, seeking the coveted, narcissistically invested designation "training and supervising analyst." In addition, he may seek positions of prominence within local and national professional organizations. Each of these achievements alters his self-representation and temporarily restores to it an illusion of narcissistic perfection.

What factors within contemporary psychoanalysis have complemented the intrapsychic factors I have described to motivate some colleagues to propose new paradigms? The consistent awareness of the therapeutic limits of psychoanalysis has led its practitioners to seek modifications that would yield more favorable results, while at the same time they have been progressively less willing to accept biologic and energic explanations for treatment failures. These factors combined with efforts to "widen the scope of psychoanalysis" (Stone,

[1] It is of interest that some of our most creative colleagues are special in that they are not physicians. How this affects their "initiation" into the psychoanalytic profession and its interminable narcissistic investments, gratifications, frustrations, and conflicts is an important question that is beyond the data available to me and the scope of this book.

1954) have generated questions concerning the role of the personality of the analyst in the analytic process (Strachey, 1934; Alexander and French, 1948; Loewald, 1960; G. Klein, 1976; Kohut, 1977). What part does interpretation of conflict play in the analytic process, and how does the role of identification with the analyst and his functions contribute to structural change? How much is structural change related to an increase in the ego's synthetic function acquired by the internalization of cognitively grounded interpretations, and how much is the analysand's ego altered by its interdigitation with a new object, the analyst, providing a new substrate to an ever-developing ego? Perhaps a more ephemeral and yet no less important question: How do these factors complement each other? The work of such analysts as Jacobson (1954), Melanie Klein (1959), Bergler (1961), Mahler et al. (1975), Kernberg (1975), and Kohut (1971, 1977) have also questioned the primacy of oedipal conflicts in the genesis of the infantile neurosis, as well as the relative importance of nurture versus nature.

Practicing analysts derive a sense of security and well-being from performing well within an established, narcissistically invested paradigm. The "classical" paradigm has provided a framework where verbal interpretation, reconstruction, and working through of an oedipal conflict and its associated infantile neurosis is most fulfilling to the analyst. The changing nature of psychoanalytic practice requires greater use of "modifications" (Stone, 1954) or "parameters" (Eissler, 1953), and this may be associated with feelings of diminished self-esteem. Analysts seek a theory that can allow them to feel secure and to derive positive self-esteem without feeling they must apologize for what they do by labeling it a "parameter."

Such feelings have contributed to a period of uncertainty in psychoanalysis where paradigms compete for analysts' attention, admiration, and fealty. In this paradigm alteration and competition, some analysts have chosen to work within the established paradigm; others, to challenge the established order. Mahler's (et al., 1975) work characterizes the former; Kohut's (1977), the latter, while Gedo and Goldberg's (1973) assumes an intermediate position. Mahler's work is revolutionary in the *shift of emphasis* she places on preoedipal factors, the role of the environment, and the importance of the vicissitudes of aggression in the genesis of character development. She accomplishes this without seriously threatening practitioners of the established paradigm by explicitly stating her allegiance to Freud, by acknowledging a biological basis to behavior ("in part intrinsic," 1975, p. 95), and by working within and thereby preserving the language of the established paradigm. This last factor is important for two very different reasons; first, it preserves the possibility of communication between analysts who disagree, and second, technical terms are important narcissistically invested ingredients of a paradigm. The practitioner derives a sense of security and positive self-esteem by exhibiting his expertise with these terms to his patients, to his colleagues, and to himself.

Mahler begins her 1972 paper with a clear statement of her allegiance to Freud: "I have based this presentation upon two thoughts of Freud – two pillars of psychoanalytic metapsychology" (p. 333). These two pillars are man's dependency upon his mother and the resulting object-relations perspective. For Freud, these pillars are relatively peripheral to the edifice he erects; for Mahler, they are central, a profoundly important shift of emphasis.

The revolutionary nature of the 1975 book slowly emerges. To begin with, radical statements are tentatively rendered in footnotes or parentheses. The foundations of ego development, defenses, and superego development *may* be found in characterological rapprochement solutions rather than in oedipal-conflict resolution. In a footnote she notes: "Whether this affective reaction could or should be regarded at such an early age as identification with the aggressor or as projective identification we do not know" (p. 97). In a parenthesis she refers to "the internalization process, which could be inferred, . . . of rules and demands (beginnings of superego)" (p. 101). These tentative suggestions become revolutionary postulates in the concluding section of her book: "One of the main yields of our study was the finding that the infantile neurosis may have its obligatory precursor, if not its first manifestation, in the rapprochement crisis" (p. 227). It is important to emphasize that, although Mahler's contribution is revolutionary in its shift of emphasis, she has, by working within the established paradigm and communicating in its language, contributed to its evolutionary development.

Gedo and Goldberg's explicit purpose in *Models of the Mind* is to help analysts deemphasize their overvaluation of any particular psychoanalytic theory. Their contribution derives, in part, from their implicit awareness of analysts' penchant for a tenacious and interminable narcissistic investment of paradigms. Their implicit purpose, which is never stated, is to facilitate the acceptance of the psychology of the self, rather than the structural hypothesis, as the main model for organizing the vast majority of analytic data. They attempt to achieve this goal by employing a number of tactics of covert paradigm competition—covert because they do not explicitly say their paradigm is any better than any other paradigm.

Their first ingenious tactic is to introduce a systems-theory orientation borrowed from the hard sciences. The concept of "theoretical complementarity" (p. 4) allows them to establish logically that "all models are of equal importance" (p. 9). They distinguish models from the theories they represent and state: "A model is a tool, and one tool is no better than another, although in performing a specific task certain tools are more useful than others" (p. 9).

Gedo and Goldberg (1973) propose a hierarchical model

that allows the analyst to maintain the illusion he is giving up nothing. He can retain the tripartite, topographic, reflex-arc models in his armentarium of narcissistically invested models and add a new one, the psychology of the self. In addition, they transform definitions that have held meaning for post-Freudian ego psychology without defining the fact, or the purpose, of their change. For example, their use of the term *maturation* (p. 16) is different from Hartmann's (1950a) and blurs the distinction he drew between maturation and development.

They define the tripartite model in a manner that limits it to the organization of the data of intersystemic conflict that Freud emphasizes in *The Ego and the Id* (1923a). It is important to note that Gedo and Goldberg choose the tripartite model rather than the structural hypothesis, for, as I am suggesting, the evolving structural hypothesis offers a model for much more than the organization of data of intersystemic conflict. It also easily accommodates data that reflect intrasystemic conflict and the traumatic influences of real parental objects – data which Gedo, Goldberg, and Kohut suggest require new paradigms to comprehend.

In addition to limiting the meaning of the structural hypothesis, Gedo and Goldberg devalue the subsequent contributions of Freud and of post-Freudian elaborators. Often these deemphasizing remarks occur in footnotes. I stress this point because a reader who is caught up in the search for a new paradigm to narcissistically invest will be less motivated to read a footnote. The limited definition of the tripartite model dissociates it from Freud's (1926) own subsequent ego-psychological elaborations, as well as from those of Waelder (1930), Anna Freud (1936), Hartmann (1939), Jacobson (1954), Arlow and Brenner (1964), and Mahler. They justify this by considering "ego psychology" to have "burst the confines of the original Freudian conceptualizations contained in *The Ego and the Id*" (p. 53). They ignore the profoundly important shifts of emphasis in Waelder's (1930) concept "assimilation" (p. 48) and Hartmann's concept adaptation. The ego and its active adaptational quest for synthesis and integration are central to these conceptualizations; id discharge and tension reduction are clearly of secondary significance. In their effort to emphasize the importance of Kohut, they disparage, in a footnote, the evolutionary perspective in general and the contributions of Jacobson in particular: "Jacobson (1964) *manages* to discuss the same subject using the terminology of ego psychology" (p. 184, emphasis added). Finally, they distort fact in the body of their text and correct this in footnotes: "Ferenczi (1913). . . constructed the first psychoanalytic line of development.[10]" But in footnote 10 they state: "Actually, Freud had implied the line of development of the libido in *Three Essays on the Theory of Sexuality* (1905), but the substages of this line were not spelled out until later" (p. 185). It would seem reasonable to translate this footnote to read, "Freud proposed the line of development of the libido, which was subsequently elaborated." Gedo and Goldberg – and Kohut (1977, p. 301) in his emphasis on the role of Breuer as the discoverer of psychoanalysis – are attempting to deemphasize the significance of Freud's original contributions to psychoanalysis in order to facilitate a mobility of narcissistic investments in Freud and his metapsychology.

It is beyond the scope of this chapter to deal critically with competing paradigms; however, it is worth noting that both Kohut (1977) and Shafer (1976) have been influenced by Kuhn and narcissistically invest their own contributions.

Schafer (1976) refers to Kuhn's 1970 article as a theoretical justification for his "revolutionary" confrontation of ego psychology. From a Kuhnian perspective, Schafer (1976, p. 178) describes Erikson, Kohut (his earlier work), and Mahler as "major figure[s] of this transitional phase" (p. 179) in reorienting psychoanalytic theory. He conceptualizes the adaptive ego (Hartmann), identity, and self to be "stopgap" concepts at-

tempting "to reintroduce the . . . 'I' into metapsychology" (p.
112). Schafer's perspective suggests that he believes psychoanalysis requires a radical revision in its language to properly
integrate the "I" into its theory and that his "action language"
is that paradigmatic alternative.

Kohut (1977) compares himself to Freud as Kuhn might
have compared Bohr or Heisenberg to Newton: "I will add
here that [there are] parallelisms between the development of
physics from Newtonian theory to quantum theory [Bohr,
Heisenberg] and the development of psychoanalysis from
Freudian metapsychology to the psychology of the self" (p.
31n.). Ornstein (1978, p. 92) quotes Kuhn directly and employs
Kuhn's concept of "normal vs. revolutionary science" to advo-
cate his view of Kohut's paradigm as "new" (p. 105). Of others,
he states: "The overwhelming number of significant contributions in our field have merely kept psychoanalysis on the same
path; in the sense of 'normal science,' there have only been
corrections, improvements, expansions, and minor or major
changes of the *existing* paradigm" (p. 105).

In exploring the nature of Kohut's (1977) work as an example of overt and revolutionary paradigm competition, I have
stressed that it is not only beyond the scope of this chapter,
but that it is not its purpose, to critically review his *very
valuable* contribution. I have presented my views of his work
in the paper "Toward a Critique of the Psychology of the Self."
That critique is written from the evolutionary perspective being elaborated in this book to mitigate what this author considers to be unnecessary aspects of paradigm competition and
to facilitate the integration of valuable aspects of Kohut's contribution into an evolving structural hypothesis and an evolving psychoanalytic technique.

Kohut's descriptions of ubiquitous countertransference responses to narcissistic transference phenomena are particularly relevant in the context of elaborating an evolutionary
perspective on paradigm development. All creators' contribu-

tions are limited by a number of factors including the limits deriving from their personalities, their countertransference potentials at the time of their contributions. Kohut (1971) describes, and Gedo (1975) elaborates upon, the countertransference response of premature and defensive disavowal of an analysand's delegated idealization when working within the process of an idealizing transference. This is particularly important because of Freud's probable unawareness of this countertransference potential within himself and its influence on his view of psychoanalytic process:

> Perhaps it may depend, too, on whether the personality of the analyst allows of the patients' putting him in the place of his ego ideal, and this involves a temptation for the analyst to play the part of prophet, saviour redeemer to the patient. Since the rules of analysis are diametrically opposed to the physician's making use of his personality in any such manner, it must be honestly confessed that here we have another limitation to the effectiveness of analysis [Freud, 1923a, p. 50n.].

Kohut's delineation of the analyst's discomfort in response to the "patient's putting him in the place of his ego ideal" as a countertransference response reflecting unresolved conflicts concerning exhibitionistic wishes is a significant contribution to the evolving theory of analytic technique, as well as to the analysts' ability to engender the regression implicit in facilitating the establishment of the idealizing aspect of a transference neurosis and in interpreting its defensive function at appropriate moments of an analytic process.

There has been a transition from Kohut's original attempt to work within ego psychology to his present revolutionary effort to create a new paradigm. It should be noted that most of the earlier substantive criticism of his work has been directed at his theoretical rather than his clinical contributions and particularly at his concept of an "independent line of narcissistic libido" rather than at what I (1980b) have suggested may be his more enduring contribution. One might speculate that the validity of his insights provokes anxiety that motivates some to disparage his contributions by criticizing them on a tangential issue, that of narcissistic libido. It also seems reasonable to speculate that the criticism and rejection of aspects of his work have contributed to his decision to reject the established paradigm and propose a new one. More recent criticisms of his work have focused increasingly on his descriptions of technique. Many colleagues, including this author, suggest that despite his disavowal, Kohut is increasingly advocating a variety of a corrective emotional experience.

As difficult as these speculations are to consider it may be that it is just such emotional issues that inevitably influence paradigm competition when the narcissistic investment of paradigms remains unconscious or significantly unassimilated.

At any rate, Kohut (1977) clearly disavows the established psychoanalytic paradigm: "I have come to recognize the limits of the applicability of some basic analytic formulations.... The classical psychoanalytic conceptualization of the nature of man ... does not do justice to a broad band in the spectrum of human psychopathology and to a great number of other psychological phenomena we encounter outside the clinical situation" (p. xviii). By such advocacy he isolates his work from related efforts of other analysts because, in his view, their results have "been obtained by approaches that are consistent with viewpoints that are different from mine, or that had been formulated within a vague, ambiguous, or shifting theoretical framework" (p. xxi).

This is an example of paradigm grandiosity. Kohut's (1977) recent book contains numerous signs of this kind of overvaluation: "Heightened and lowered self-esteem ... dejection and rage at frustration ... can be understood only within the framework of the psychology of the self" (pp. 191–192). In addition to this exclusive emphasis on his own theory Kohut seems to conceive of his contributions as the savior of psychoanalysis. They are needed "if it wants to stay alive" (p. 268). Finally, in creating a new paradigm, Kohut has given old words new meanings without discussing this as a fact and without discussing the merits of such changes, i.e., "self-object" (p. 32), as well as "defensive" (p. 3), and "compensatory" (p. 3) narcissistic investments. His 1977 book proposes to change the commonly accepted meanings of the analytic situation, process, and termination, as well as of the oedipal period of development.

Ultimately the validity of a theory will rest upon its value in the clinical situation. Nevertheless, in the heat and rancor that sometimes accompany paradigm competition, analysts often resort to pejorative interpretation of their colleagues' inability to see the validity of their contributions. Such interpretation is rarely welcomed and interferes with communication.

Bergler (1961), who has written prolifically and meaningfully on masochism, conceives of it as the unifactorial foundation of all human suffering: *"I believe that there exists ONE basic neurosis, acquired in the first eighteen months of life: psychic masochism. All later neurotic manifestations of a libidinous – pseudoaggressive nature are only rescue stations* to hide the basic conflict" (p. 18). Many colleagues have been repelled by his style and critical of what they consider his simplistic reductionism, a situation not dissimilar to the one Kohut has created for himself. Bergler interprets the rejection of his work as his colleagues' narcissistic defense against perceiving their unconscious longing for masochistic gratifications (p. 142).

In a similar manner Kohut describes the limits of Freud's personality on his theory building, as well as the defensive function for contemporary Freudians served by residual idealization of Freud and his contributions. In the epilogue to his 1977 book, Kohut considers the "influence of Freud's personality" (p. 290). He suggests that Freud's vision is limited by his: "inability to see himself as great [and] related symptoms such as his embarrassment at being looked at" (pp. 292–293). Kohut continues, "I have no doubt [that Freud's personality manifests] a sharply circumscribed vulnerability – to be exact: a fear of overstimulation in the narcissistic sector, in the area of exhibitionism" (p. 294). Kohut labels these aspects of Freud's personality a "defect" (p. 294) and then undoes this denigration: "Freud's limitation . . . should not be evaluated as a defect but as a characteristic feature of his personality" (p. 295).

Kohut (1976) interprets contemporary colleagues' idealization of Freud as a defense against the experience of "envy, jealousy and rage":

> If the present-day psychoanalyst can maintain that everything of importance in psychoanalysis has already been said by Freud, if, furthermore, the imago of Freud has been securely included in the analyst's idealized superego and has thus become a part of the self, then he can disregard contemporary competitors, they are not a threat to his own narcissistic security, and he can avoid suffering the painful narcissistic injuries that the comparison with the actual rivals for the goals of his narcissistic strivings might inflict on him [p. 802].

There is truth in Kohut's observations on Freud and on his own contemporary colleagues. However, in the context of paradigm competition, Kohut's comments can be understood to reflect his effort to facilitate the "deidealization" (p. 802) of Freud and the compensatory narcissistic investment of Kohut. Paradoxically the opposite effect obtains; readers are offended, rational discourse is impeded, and polemical paradigmatic responses are often engendered.

Whatever the influence of Breuer, Fliess, nineteenth-century Western civilization and its scientific perspectives, etc., had on Freud, he was a genius who, like all geniuses, transcended his time. However imperfect Freud's scientific contributions, all contemporary and future analysts will have to respond to the narcissistic injury that Freud was the first psychoanalyst. Nevertheless, in the spirit of pursuit of a more objective reality, the interests of our science justify inquiry into the limits and irrational motives of all theoreticians, particularly when this may elucidate the meaning and the inevitably limited value of a particular contribution.

This chapter has discussed Kohut's overvaluation of his "broader" psychology of the self. It is worth considering how the inevitable limits of Kohut's personality have contributed to his deemphasizing the importance of aggression, of rage, in the human situation. Inevitably these paradigmatic constructs are limited in their applications to the clinical situation. While acknowledging the potential usefulness of not prematurely interpreting an analysand's delegated idealization, I am suggesting that Kohut's perspective has influenced him to develop a theory and technique that facilitates the avoidance of the conscious experience of conflict and rage by engendering a defensive idealization of the analyst. This defensive identification process he terms "compensatory transmuting internalizations." These shape the emerging "oedipal constellations as new; . . . they are a positive result of a consolidation of the self never before achieved" (1977, p. 228). Kohut justifies his thesis by pointing out that "the analysand experiences the terminal oedipal phase in these instances almost entirely in terms of fantasies about the analyst and the analyst's family" (p. 228). It seems reasonable to suggest that these internalizations represent the result of unnecessary and unanalyzed transference gratification. In that regard Loewald (1973) has suggested that Kohut's work may suffer from a countertransference overvaluation of narcissism: "Kohut's seeming neglect of analytic work with this type of resistance leads to the impression that a subtle kind of seduction of the patient may be at play in his work with such disorders" (p. 448). "An overidentification with the patient's narcissistic needs . . . is . . . uncalled for. It is my impression that Kohut is not sufficiently aware of or concerned with this . . . problem" (pp. 445–446).

I (1980b) have suggested that this factor has contributed

to Kohut's developing a treatment referred to as "analysis" within the theory of the psychology of the self. From the perspective of the structural hypothesis and the corollary emphasis on the primary importance of interpretation and insight in the mode of therapeutic action of analysis the technique Kohut advocates is considered a supportive psychotherapy.

Kuhn emphasizes that the belief that paradigms are creations of individuals is a distortion of reality, an illusion: "Discovery is a process and must take time" (1962, p. 55). He adds that "in principle, a new phenomenon might emerge without reflecting destruction on any part of past scientific practice" (p. 95). Narcissistic investments are an interminable aspect of the human condition. To the degree these investments can be diminished the perception of reality is enhanced. This is always a relative process. So also with paradigms – the relative divestment of the narcissistic investment of paradigms and their "creators" will contribute to the reduction of irrational polemical aspects of paradigm competition. If paradigms are significantly divested of their narcissistic investment, a science might experience a process more akin to Hegelian dialectic (1837) than to Kuhnian revolution. Paradigms could then be viewed as imperfect and improvable. This view contributes to a situation where analysts with different points of view can employ one language with which to discuss their differences. From this perspective the structural hypothesis serves as a supraordinate frame of reference encompassing a number of complementary and resonant models. At this time psychoanalysis as an evolving science and therapeutic method is better served if opportunities for communication are maximized by discussing issues relating to the development and pathology of the self-representation (Hartmann, 1950a), self-image (Sandler, 1960), the self in the "narrow" and "broader" sense (G. Klein, 1976; Kohut, 1977), as well as issues of self-esteem as aspects of the structural hypothesis. The second section of this book pursues this goal.

# Part II

## A Contemporary Understanding
## of the
## Structural Hypothesis

*It would seem that a number of difficult theoretical problems can be resolved provided we do not set out on investigation with too rigid preconceptions as to psychic structure.*

Edward Glover, "Grades of Ego Differentiation"

# CHAPTER 2

# The Ego

*Many misunderstandings and unclarities are traceable*
*to the fact that we have not yet trained ourselves to con-*
*sider the ego from an intrasystemic point of view.*
Heinz Hartmann
"Comments on the Psychoanalytic Theory of the Ego"

An increasing number of analysts are criticizing Freud's
metapsychology in general and his structural hypothesis in
particular. In addition, a number of these critics are proposing
new psychoanalytic paradigms and espousing the advantages
of their constructs for organizing the data of the psychoanalytic situation.

I believe that the structural hypothesis remains eminently
useful and that its usefulness is enhanced if it is viewed from
an evolutionary perspective. Freud's constructs constantly
evolve in response to both his awareness of their ineluctable
imperfections and his increasing clinical experience. Inevitably one or another aspect of his work receives emphasis at a
particular era in the development of psychoanalytic metapsychology. The early emphasis of Freud's work is on the delineation of the unconscious, part of which is subsequently referred
to as the id. His increasing analytic experience, his discovery
and delineation of transference, and particularly his struggle
to understand man's irrational penchant for pursuits "beyond
the pleasure principle" lead him to reformulate his conception
of the mental apparatus. In *The Ego and the Id* he states: "The
present discussions are a further development of some trains

31

of thought which I opened up in *Beyond the Pleasure Principle*. . . . It stands closer to psychoanalysis. . . . It is more in the nature of synthesis" (p. 12). In this synthesis he raises the concept of the ego to a metapsychological construct that will progressively occupy analysts' attention. From 1923 until the present time Freud's functional definition of the ego has been emphasized and elaborated. The most seriously considered new paradigms – those of George Klein (1976), Schafer (1976), and Kohut (1977) – have derived, in part, from these colleagues' critical views of the functional definition of the ego and their belief that psychoanalysis requires a new paradigm organized around the self (Klein and Kohut) or the "I" (Schafer). Such criticisms have validity but do not justify these authors' radical solutions. Instead, I propose that an elaboration of Freud's *developmental* and *representational* definitions of the ego as a complement to his functional definition provides a more balanced emphasis and preserves the theoretical and clinical usefulness of the structural hypothesis.

Kohut (1977), Schafer (1976), and George Klein (1976) have proposed new psychoanalytic paradigms. Kohut's (1971, 1972) original efforts to work within the established psychoanalytic paradigm have evolved into his more recent effort to propose a new paradigm. This metamorphosis is characterized by a transitional period during which his colleagues have criticized Freud's metapsychology. Basch (1973) centers on the disadvantages of the economic point of view. Gedo and Goldberg (1973) propose a hierarchic model of "theoretical complementarity" (p. 4) to facilitate the acceptance of the psychology of the self. To do so they limit the definition of the structural hypothesis to that Freud gave it in *The Ego and the Id:* "When the formation of the superego ends the requirement for the participation of an outside person in the child's self regulation, the self-object model ceases to be the most relevant one for the classification of behavior. Through the phases in which intrapsychic conflicts succeed separation or castration anxieties as the typical dangers, the tripartite or topographic models are most applicable" (p. 79). Because I (1980c) have devoted a paper to a critique of the psychology of the self, I will do no more in this chapter than to reiterate Kohut's (1977) position of having "come to recognize the limits of the applicability of some of the basic analytic formulations" (p. xviii) while proposing that a great deal of human experience in general and of the psychoanalytic situation in particular "can be understood *only* within the framework of the psychology of the self" (pp. 191–192, emphasis added).

After considerable effort to work within established metapsychology, Schafer (1976) proposes "action language" as a "clinically useful and systematic alternative to metapsychology." He believes this is essential because of the "mechanistic and anthropomorphic modes of thought that are essential and correlative aspects of metapsychological conceptualization" (p. xi). His criticism of Freud and Hartmann is that they chose a "natural science" (p. 86) model of the mind: "This approach excludes meaning from the center of psychoanalytic theory. It deals with meaning only by changing it to something else (functions, energies, 'principles,' etc.). But meaning (and intention) is the same as 'psychic reality'" (p. 100). Schafer believes a theory is required that is closer to experience, that focuses upon the individual with respect and affirmation and that conceives of each human being as responsible for actively creating his or her situation. Schafer believes this requires a theory that derives from a view of the subject as an "I." He believes that the concept of the representational world as it exists in traditional metapsychology does not facilitate such an emphasis:

> From the point of view of traditional theory, the *self*-representation refers merely to one kind of mental content; though a necessary concept, it is not central [p. 115].

Further:

> Rather than their being viewed as types of representations,
> self and identity are commonly treated as motivational-struc-
> tural entities on the order of 'the ego' in which regard they
> suffer the same reification that has afflicted Freud's concepts
> of psychic structure. Thus self and identity have been spoken
> of as though they are spaces, places, substances, agencies, in-
> dependent minds, forces and so forth [p. 193].

His "action language" is a means to exorcise mechanisms,
energies, and anthropomorphisms from psychoanalytic jargon. Action language "speaks of intentions, meanings, reasons, or subjective experience" (p. 103); "emotions are done
not had" (p. 357).

As has been noted in Chapter 1, Kohut (1977) and Schafer
(1976) have been influenced by and accept Kuhn's view of
revolutionary process in science and see themselves as revolutionary figures in relation to Freud.

Although George Klein (1976) has an evolutionary view of
the process of the development of psychoanalytic theory,
there is much in common between his and Schafer's substantive criticisms of metapsychology. Klein believes that metapsychology suffers from "obscurantist jargon . . . the dry rot
of overconceptualization" (p. 13). He proposes that within "the
so-called 'structural point of view' the ego has lost is distinc-
tiveness as a clinical psychoanalytic concept" (p. 7) and that
"there are grave doubts about its viability as a *theory, in its
present form*" (p. 150).

The first of three areas of "irresolution within ego psychology . . . is whether the ego is an entity or a classification"
(p. 150). In his criticism of Freud, he, like Schafer and Kohut,
is concerned with the lack of an "explicit recognition of 'self'
as a grade of ego organization with distinctive organizing
functions and motivations" (p. 139), and points out that "the
ego's functions in the positive role of creator, rather than as
defender or adjuster, were only hinted at" (p. 139). His second

criticism of ego psychology concerns the "ambiguity of the ego's relation to drive" (p. 153). In this regard he objects to the concept of a "blind drive energy . . . independent of controls" (p. 154). Finally he is critical of explanations in terms of "process" rather than of "motivation" and, like Schafer, believes this difficulty derives from the energic point of view.

In regard to Freud's work he proposes what he considers to be a radical shift of emphasis that will result in a reformulation of Freud's "inductively derived major clinical propositions" (p. 5). Like Freud (1923a), Klein returns to *Beyond the Pleasure Principle* to find the organizing nidus for his shift of emphasis. He notes Freud's energic and traumatic explanations for behavior organized "beyond the pleasure principle" and speculates that had Freud emphasized the latter rather than the former, "had he stayed with the initial formulation the outline of a truly dynamic ego psychology might have evolved from *Beyond the Pleasure Principle*" (p. 263). Klein, like Mahler, Kohut, and Schafer, emphasizes the importance of traumatic environmental influences on ego development: "In retrospect the seduction theory was only an overstatement of a more seminal insight: the critical nature of conflicted wish involving a willful parental influence, the theme of exploitation of young by old" (p. 164). His stress on the role of the environment leads him to a representational view of character: "The resolution of an incompatibility takes the form of a cognitive emotional schema . . . an *internal structured altered direction* of *motivation* and *aim* . . . an internal environment . . . of rules and relationships" (pp. 166–167). He conceives of conflicts, not in terms of "*inherent* conflict of forces" but in terms of "self-integration." Waelder's concept of "assimilation" is not sufficient; conflict should be seen as a failure of "self-integration," and "an integrating center *beyond* the ego" (p. 171) is necessary.

It is characteristic of Freud's seminal articles that they offer a variety of definitions for central concepts such as the ego. His functional definition has been emphasized and elaborated, but other definitions provide a basis for the elaboration of the concept of the representational world as a more significant aspect of the ego.

The functional definition of the ego is emphasized in the energic metaphor of *The Project.* Freud presents the ego as developing to control and modulate discharge in response to "the exigencies of life": "A primary neuronic system, having thus acquired a quantity (Qn), employs it only in order to get rid of it through the connecting path leading to the muscular mechanism, and thus keeps itself free from stimulus. This *function* of discharge is the primary function of neuronic systems" (p. 357, emphasis added). In response to the perception of frustrating reality, the neuronic system develops a "secondary function" that results in "specific actions" aimed at more effective and adaptive discharge. Freud elaborates perception, memory, and reality testing as components of this "secondary function."

In *The Ego and the Id,* through the often quoted simile of a man on horseback, Freud presents a relatively weak ego that functions as mediator between the "passions" (p. 25) of the id and the constraints of reality: "It [the ego] is intrusted with important functions. By virtue of its relation to the perceptual system it gives mental processes an order in time and submits them to 'reality testing.' By interposing the processes of thinking, it secures a postponement of motor discharge and controls the access to motility" (p. 55).

In the prestructural language of Chapter 7 of *The Interpretation of Dreams,* Freud presents a definition of "character" that presages the representational perspective being emphasized here: "What we describe as our 'character' is based on the memory-traces of our impressions; and, moreover, the impressions which have the greatest effect on us – those of our earliest youth – are precisely the ones which scarcely ever become conscious" (pp. 539–540).

In *Mourning and Melancholia*, Freud (1917a) presents a modern object-relations explanation of mourning, melancholia, mania, obsessional neurosis, and hysterical identification, as well as of narcissistic regression, identification, and object choice. Because of the transitional nature of this paper in Freud's theory building, processes that will later be discussed almost exclusively as vicissitudes of oral incorporative, defensive identifications of the ego in response to narcissistic injury are here discussed from the energic perspective of secondary narcissism as "regression of libido into the ego" (p. 258). Freud clearly demonstrates his view of the ego as representational world and presages Schafer's (1968) concept "self-as-object" (p. 80). "The analysis of melancholia now shows that *the ego can . . . treat itself as an object*" (Freud, 1917a, emphasis added). In relationship to the representational struggle of the manic patient, he states: "The manic subject plainly demonstrates his liberation from the object" (p. 255).

In *The Ego and the Id,* Freud explicitly elaborates a representational definition of ego:

> The ego is that part of id which has been modified by the direct influence of the external world. . . . An object cathexis has been replaced by an identification. . . . This kind of substitution has a great share in determining the form taken by the ego and . . . it makes an essential contribution towards building up what is called its 'character.' . . . The character of the ego is a precipitate abandoned object cathexis and . . . it contains the history of those object-choices [pp. 25, 28, 29].

In the half-century since the introduction of the structural point of view, its elaboration has focused on and emphasized the delineation of the functional perspective. Anna Freud (1936) points to a shift of interest from the study of the id to that of the ego. The emphasis of her view of the ego, however, is instinctual. From this perspective, she elaborates the ego's defensive function: "In analysis *all* the material which assists us to analyze the ego makes its appearance in the form of resistance to the analysis of the id" (p. 32, emphasis added). Toward the end of the book, the focus shifts to such defensive processes involving the representational world as "identification with the aggressor": "Identification . . . combines with other mechanisms to form one of the ego's most potent weapons in dealing with external objects which arose its anxiety" (p. 117).

In 1936 Waelder publishes another classic of ego psychology. Waelder extends the concept of the ego's integrative and synthetic function. The ego does not just respond to the id, the superego, or the compulsion to repeat, "but in addition it assigns to *itself* definite problems, such as overcoming the other agencies or joining them to its organization by active assimilation" (p. 48).

Waelder's delineation of the ego's assimilative function results in a functional, in contrast to Freud's (1923a) representational, definition of character. However, the active aspect of the assimilative function suggests the "I" or "agent" quality that Klein and Schafer have emphasized. As such it forms a bridge between a functional and representational view of the ego. As Waelder states: "The ego . . . represents the considered direction of man, all purposeful activity. . . . The ego always faces problems and seeks to find their solutions. Each of man's actions has in every case to pass through the ego and is thus an attempt to solve a problem" (pp. 45–46). Thus "character is very largely determined through specific solution methods which are peculiar to each individual" (pp. 52–53).

In a similar fashion, Hartmann (1939), from a functional perspective, emphasizes the agent quality of the ego and portrays it as a structure with its own goals. "The synthetic function" reflects the ego as a "specific organ of adaptation . . . not merely [as] a resultant of other forces" (p. 39). In "Comments on the Psychoanalytic Theory of the Ego," his effort to expand our appreciation of the ego as a functional apparatus, he delineates Freud's two uses of the term *ego*. Hartmann notes that Freud uses the term to refer to self and to a set of functions. Hartmann elaborates the self-representation as part of the representational world and the ego as "a substructure of the personality... defined by its functions" (1950a, p. 75). Jacobson (1964) has expanded Hartmann's distinction between the "concepts of the self and self representations (analogous to object representation) as distinct from that of the ego" (p. 19).

In order to elaborate a distinction between identification and introjection, Sandler and Rosenblatt (1962) focus on the representational world as an aspect of ego: "We have found it necessary to distinguish between the ego as a structure or organized set of functions on the one hand, and the representational world on the other" (p. 133). They proceed to delineate the development of the self-representation via processes of perception, identification, and differentiation, as well as the development of object representations via processes of internalization. They conceive of the superego as definitively emerging at the oedipal stage of development via processes of introjection. In addition, they delineate a concept of the "ideal self" (p. 136). Because of their fealty to Hartmann's orientation, the representational world is presented *solely* as a *passive* content of the mental apparatus that is strictly *subordinate* to the ego as a set of functions:

> It is important to delineate the relation between the representational world and the ego. It is a function of the ego to construct a representational world from the original undifferentiated sensorium of the infant, ... for the building up of representations is a sine qua non for ego development, and is itself a prerequisite for progressive adaptation. *In this the ego is and remains the active agency. The representational world is never an active agent.* It is rather a set of indications which guides the ego to appropriate adaptive or defensive activity [p. 136, emphasis added].

Schafer, despite his subsequent disavowal (1976), has made what I believe is a valuable contribution to the elaboration of the representational world as an aspect of the ego. He distinguishes identification and introjection as different processes of internalization defined by their position in the representational world. His definitions of "the self-as-agent (the 'I') and the self-as-object (the 'me')" (1968, p. 80) offer a valuable elaboration of the structural hypothesis that facilitates the organization of experience reflective of intrasystemic conflict.

A distinction is usually made between metapsychology and clinical theory when discussing psychoanalytic theory. Freud's style of proposing multiple definitions and explanations for an event lend credence to this distinction; for example, his instinctual and dynamic-traumatic explanations of behavior that he conceptualizes as "beyond the pleasure principle." Most critics of Freud refer to theories that are steeped in mechanistic metaphor as metapsychology and to theories that are constructed in language closer to behavioral data as clinical theories. In this chapter all theories will be referred to as metapsychology. In a similar fashion to Basch (1973), a theory will be defined as an inductive hypothesis derived from introspection or "free floating" empathic observation. The concept of a clinical theory will refer to the rules of analysis. For example, although following the suggestions of Freud (1923a) and Arlow and Brenner (1964), one might no longer employ the topographic model of the mind, Chapter 7 of *The Interpretation of Dreams* continues to be referred to as a rich source of clinical dream theory. Freud's description of nodal points in dreams, of the management of resistance in general and of doubt and forgetting in particular, as well as his technical suggestions to a patient to repeat a dream, are still of considerable heuristic value (pp. 515–518).

A unitary definition of metapsychology carries a number of advantages. If a particular analyst is disenchanted with the energic point of view, he need not cease to use the entire structural model of the mind. Relatively minor translations of energic metaphors clarify material that may seem obscure. For example, the term *investment* can be substituted for the term *cathexis*. Such minor effort seems a small price to pay in order to facilitate students' ease of access to Freud's seminal contributions. In fact, if one considers Freud's energic statements as metaphors a number of superficially energic propositions suggest rich representational implications.

In *The Ego and the Id,* Freud proposes that "we should like to learn more about the ego now that we know it, too, can be unconscious in the proper sense of the word" (p. 19). From a functional perspective Hartmann (1950a) indicates the necessity of studying "intrasystemic *conflicts*" (p. 93, emphasis added) of the ego:

> I have mentioned ego functions opposing each other. Because these conflicts are not of the same relevance as those between the ego and the id, or the ego and reality, etc., we are not used to thinking of them in terms of conflicts and thus distinguish them from those other, better known conflicts that we may designate intersystemic. The intrasystemic correlations and conflicts have hardly ever been consistently studied . . . many misunderstandings and unclarities are traceable to the fact that we have not yet trained ourselves to consider the ego from an intrasystemic point of view. One speaks of 'the ego' as being rational, or realistic, or an integrator, while actually those are characteristics of one or the other of its functions only [p. 93].

This chapter proposes that conceptualizing the ego as composed of a variety of substructures facilitates the systematic study of intrasystemic conflicts. Traditionally, the representational world has been conceptualized as *solely* a passive, reified content that is subsumed within the functions of the ego and is subordinate to it. This paper proposes a *shift of emphasis* that conceptualizes the representational world as a substructure of the ego of equal importance to the ego functions and importantly related to them.

The representational world is a rich panoply of self- and object representations in ever changing states of integration. They are affectively laden; may be archaically elaborated and narcissistically, masochistically, or sadistically invested; and may be felt to possess varying degrees of activity or passivity. Activity, the subjective feeling of "I" or "agent," is just one more, albeit very important, potential content (conscious or unconscious) of representations. Federn (1928), like Schafer, suggests that "the ego must be conceived of as a continuous experience of the psyche and not as a conceptual abstraction" (p. 283). I am suggesting that the ego can be conceived of in a variety of ways as both an experience and as an abstraction or content of the mental apparatus. The "I" experience can be conceptualized from an abstract perspective as a content of the ego and designated the self-representation-as-agent.

George Klein (1976) has suggested that "an integrating center *beyond* the ego" (p. 171) is necessary. The proposed schema allows for such an integration. Multiple self-representations exist. "Grades" or "splits" within the representational world exist and are variably maintained. The self-representation develops out of a conglomerate of preindividuated impressions that become preverbal, affectively laden, predominantly action-organized memory traces in a state of primary repression. These memory traces contribute to the narcissistically invested core of the self-representation-as-agent, the "I," that feels itself identified "with the totality" (Andreas-Salomé, 1921). Infant observation demonstrates that the neonate is active in eliciting responses from the object world. Sander (1962) has shown that neonatal patterning is influenced by both the quality of the subject's basic core (Weil, 1970) and the object. His work suggests that from earliest infancy there exists a significant interaction between the neonate's active seeking and his object world – an interaction that contributes a neurophysiologic substrate to his developing representational world. The construction of the self-representation-as-object is a later acquisition that can be roughly correlated with the toddler's developing pleasure in mirror play during the last half of the second year of life.

As development proceeds, the self-representations become progressively differentiated and hierarchically organized. A self-representation-as-agent develops that conceives of itself as existing to pursue actively and insure its well-being and survival. This representation interacts with, mobilizes, and employs aspects of the functional substructure of the ego. As ego functions mature under the influence of predetermined biological timetables and endowments and develop under the aegis of the object world, a self-representation-as-agent normally develops that organizes its pursuits in relationship to the other agencies of the mind. As the subject's ego ideal, superego, and sense of reality develop, a self-representation-as-agent develops that pursues what Freud (1911a) refers to as "the reality principle" (p. 226). However, ubiquitous "grades" within the self-representation persist, leaving narcissistically, masochistically, or sadistically invested self-representations-as-agents that pursue the "pleasure principle" (p. 219) and the "compulsion to repeat" (Freud, 1920, p. 19). These latter self-representations mobilize and employ other more primitive aspects of the functional substructure of the ego. The self-representation-as-agent that is organized in pursuit of the reality principle struggles to "assimilate" its archaic counterparts. The interminability of this assimilative effort insures the inevitability of conflict, distortion, and creativity in the human situation.

Glover (1930) comments on the representational complexity of the normal developing ego: "It is conceivable that at the stage we usually describe as that of primary identification, there are as many primary Egos as there are combinations of erotogenic zones with reactive discharge systems: in other words, it is conceivable that the so-called primitive Ego is originally a polymorphous construction" (p. 10). Freud (1923a) similarly emphasizes this representational complexity in regard to normal and pathological ego development:

> If [the ego's object identifications] obtain the upper hand and become too numerous, unduly powerful and incompatible with one another, a pathological outcome will not be far off. It may come to a disruption of the ego in consequence of the different identifications becoming cut off from one another by resistances; perhaps the secret of the cases of what is described as "multiple personality" is that *the different identifications seize hold of consciousness in turn.* Even when things do not go so far as this, there remains the question of conflicts between the various identifications into which the ego comes apart, conflicts which cannot after all be described as entirely pathological [pp. 30–31, emphasis added].

In less precise language Kohut (1971) describes one such failure of assimilation: "If optimal development and integration of the grandiose self is interfered with, however, then this psychic structure may become split off from the reality ego and/or may become separated from it by repression" (p. 108).

From a representational perspective Freud (1916b) suggests "that Shakespeare often splits a character up into two personages . . . like two disunited parts of a single psychical individuality" (pp. 323–324). Situations we refer to as pathological consist of relative failures of assimilation. Where a subject feels compelled to pursue an excess of self-destructive, perverse, narcissistic, masochistic, or sadistic goals, the self-representation-as-agent has not assimilated the traumatic influences of the subject's childhood. Analysis aims at facilitating that integration.

Freud (1916b), discussing "those wrecked by success" (p. 316), employs the literary characters Lady Macbeth and Rebecca West to illustrate failures of assimilation. Freud's use of these literary characters as "clinical examples" emphasizes the debt of psychoanalysis to the humanities. The genius of Shakespeare and Ibsen facilitates Freud's understanding and portrayal of the dramatic self-destructiveness and behavior "beyond the pleasure principle" that derives from such failures of assimilation.

Stevenson's (1886) *Dr. Jekyll and Mr. Hyde* provides a dramatic example of intrasystemic conflict between self-representations-as-agents. The essence of such intrasystemic conflict is the struggle of the respective self-representations-as-agents for control of the executive functions of the subject's ego. Dr. Jekyll's self-representation-as-agent is organized in relationship to the reality principle. He vainly struggles to assimilate his split off self-representation-as-agent that is organized according to the pleasure principle and the compulsion to repeat. Sadism, violence, and murder are Mr. Hyde's favorite pleasures. Dr. Jekyll's futile attempt to assimilate Mr. Hyde is motivated by a wish to find some sense of synchrony with his superego: an intersystemic conflict. He expresses his depressing sense of failure to resolve his intrasystemic conflict: "I thus drew steadily nearer the truth. . . . I have been doomed. . . . Man is not truly one, but truly two" (p. 79). He longs for a drug that will exorcise Mr. Hyde and solve his intrasystemic conflict: "If each, I told myself, could be housed in separate identities, life would be relieved of all that was unbearable; the unjust might go his way, . . . and the just could walk steadfastly and securely on his upward path" (p. 80). Stevenson's literary genius complements Freud's (1923a) metapsychological formulation that "the different identifications seize hold of consciousness in turn" (p. 31). Stevenson captures the poignant sense of helplessness that such subjects experience as their dissociated self-representations-as-agents alternatingly gain control of the executive functions of the ego. Of Jekyll's experience of Hyde, Stevenson notes: "He had now seen the full deformity of the creature that shared with him the phenomena of consciousness" (p. 100). Contrastingly, he states that "the hatred of Hyde for Jekyll was of a different order. His terror [of death] drove him continually to commit temporary suicide, and return to his subordinate station of a *part instead of a person*" (p. 101, emphasis added).

The functional perspective derives from an emphasis on the ego's role as controller of the id. Early in Freud's (1895) work he writes of the normative influence of the hostility of the object on ego development: "There are in the first place, objects (perceptions) which make one scream because they cause pain; . . . a perception . . . emphasizes the *hostile* character of the object and serves to direct attention to the perception. Where otherwise, owing to the pain, one would have received no clear indications of the quality of the object" (p. 423). After Freud's disillusionment with the actual seduction theory of neurosis he deemphasizes the importance of the role of the environment in the genesis of neurosis and development. In *Inhibitions, Symptoms and Anxiety,* he states: "A wolf would probably attack us irrespectively of our behavior towards it; but the loved person would not cease to love us nor should we be threatened with castration if we did not entertain certain feelings and intentions within us. Thus such instinctual impulses are determinants of external dangers and so become dangerous in themselves" (p. 145).

In a similar vein Anna Freud (1936) emphasizes the role of projection as a complementary rather than secondary mechanism in "identification with the aggressor." This instinctual perspective, as well as the distinction between the wolf and the human material object, deemphasizes the importance of the effect of the fact that a mother or father can feel (consciously or unconsciously) or even behave (as in child abuse) like a wolf.

A number of analysts concerned with alterations of ego development associated with serious character pathology have stressed the importance of the young child's perception of the enraged and sadistic parent in the genesis of these disorders. Wilhelm Reich's (1933) emphasis on "the strict mother" (p. 152) in the genesis of narcissistic character pathology and Kernberg's (1970) description of the cold enraged mothers characteristic of narcissistic personalities underline this point. Berliner (1958) stresses the role of "the illtreating parent" (p. 43) in the genesis of moral masochism. Loewenstein (1957) similarly suggests that masochistic behavior viewed from the perspective of "survival" (p. 230) rather than "drive development" is a "weapon of the weak – i.e., of every child – faced with danger of human [parental] aggression" (pp. 230–231). Identification with the aggressor can be viewed as a narcissistic and sadistic identificatory alteration of the self-representation-as-agent in response to a frightening, angry, or sadistic parent internalized and elaborated by the primary process in the developing superego. Loewenstein (1957) discovers the masochistic complement to these processes in his description of "seduction of the aggressor." He notes that "essentially it is very different than a defensive ego mechanism . . . [it] consists of behavior which seeks and frequently achieves to change an unloving to a loving attitude in the parent. And while mobilizing libido in both, *it wards off anxiety in the child and aggression in the parent*" (p. 216, emphasis added). The immature self-representation-as-agent feels its survival threatened by the murderously enraged maternal or paternal object. Such traumatic images of parents are internalized into the developing superego where the self-representation-as-agent attempts to actively master them by mobilizing a number of defensive processes. Among the important mechanisms employed by the self-representation-as-agent are defensive identificatory alterations of the self-representation. These enable the subject to feel that the dangerous superego is disarmed and that the self-representation is capable of defending itself against attack.

Freud (1913) emphasizes that an understanding of "choice" (p. 317) of defense is difficult to achieve. It may be that individuals who have had to "assimilate" the perception of the increased incidence or intensity of parental rage are more likely to "choose" identification with the aggressor as an important defensive configuration of their character armor.

One purpose of this chapter is to contribute to a more balanced view of the ego. The ego is composed of a variety of substructures among which are ego functions and the representational world. An emphasis on the functional aspect of the ego is more understandable when considering its usefulness in organizing data of the traditional neurotic. The self-representation-as-agent is implicit but not as necessary when it is functioning in relationship to a superego that is developed sufficiently to insure successful enough repression to result in inhibitions, symptoms, or anxiety in response to prohibited desires. An emphasis on the representational world is heuristic when attempting to organize data from patients experienced as more difficult and atypical – those often designated "narcissistic" or "borderline." It seems likely that patients typically considered narcissistic personality disorders and borderline personality organizations (Kernberg, 1975) have egos whose "assimilative" function is organized "beyond the pleasure principle" in compulsive, repetitive pursuits of illusions of well-being and survival. This point will be elaborated in Chapter 4.

It is probable that Wilhelm Reich's (1933), Kernberg's (1975), and Kohut's (1971, 1977) interest in working with more difficult patients has contributed to their attempts to conceptualize "character," "personality," and "the self" from a progressively more representational perspective.

This is not an all or nothing issue, and one or another perspective may be more or less useful at various moments of an analytic process. To be analyzable a subject must be judged to have an ego whose sense of reality, quality of relatedness, and capacity for trust can permit the subject to ally himself with the analyst. The traditional neurotic has less difficulty doing

this than the typical narcissistic personality disorder or masochistic character, who not uncommonly experiences the
analytic situation as excessively frustrating, perhaps even
threatening, so that it elicits paranoid ideation and defensive
activity. A representational perspective aids in conceptualizing the introductory phase as a "holding environment"
(Modell, 1976). Within such a "holding," "mirroring," or "con-
taining" ambiance a representational perspective can facilitate working with subjects, who, because of their penchant
for projection of rage and their primal experiences of enraged
and sadistic parents, often experience the analyst as critical
and potentially annihilating. These penchants frequently
result in difficult narcissistic resistances and serious acting
out, and reflect disorders of trust that may contribute to the
perpetuation of a "narcissistic misalliance" (Meissner, 1981)
within the analytic relationship. A representational perspective can contribute to the interpretation of transference
distortions deriving from intra- and intersystemic conflicts.
This can facilitate the development of "secondary trust"
(Mehlman, 1976) and a more stable therapeutic alliance so
that more analysands can reach a late midphase experience
where their egos may more frequently and consistently be
organized and function in a neurotic or normal manner.

# CHAPTER 3

# The Superego

*The initial helplessness of human beings is the* primal
source *of all* moral motives.

Sigmund Freud, *"Project for a Scientific Psychology"*

*It is the excessive severity and overpowering cruelty of
the superego, not the weakness or want of it, as it is
usually supposed, which is responsible for the behavior
of asocial and criminal persons.*

Melanie Klein

"The Early Development of Conscience in the Child"

Chapter 2 emphasizes the intrapsychic conflict of the ego;
the present chapter, taking a developmental perspective,
stresses the lifelong nature of superego development. The
superego of many, if not of most, adults is not a concisely
structured, uniformly functioning organization. Variability of
function, regression, dedifferentiation of and externalization
of structuralization, are characteristic of the superego. The
fundamental premise here, in agreement with Glover (1930)
and Mahler (et al., 1975), is that the "beginnings of superego"
(p. 101) can be correlated with the diminution of the "rapprochement struggle" and, further, that the original function
of this preoedipal superego is to provide the developing child
with an inner sense of the parents' *presence.*

   This chapter stresses preoedipal intersystemic conflict in

response to oral and anal drive derivatives as well as fixations
and distortions in the reverberation between preoedipal ego
and superego development. Excessive emphasis has been
placed on the resolution of the Oedipus complex as the most
important nodal point in superego development – and hence
on *regression* from oedipal and postoedipal integrations of
superego to preoedipal integrations in response to inter- and
intrasystemic conflict and to traumatic experiences occurring
at any stage of life. The distinction between a preoedipal
developmental arrest and a regression from oedipal conflict
to preoedipal integrations of superego is important but not always easily discerned from the data, and an analyst's theoretical orientation will influence his interpretation. For example,
what Kohut might consider data reflecting a developmental
arrest of the self, an analyst working within a more traditional perspective would be more likely to interpret as a
regression from oedipal conflict. This chapter stresses both
the preoedipal and oedipal nodal points in superego development that contribute to the resulting resonance between
modes of conflict-solving characteristic of the ego at these
various stages of development.

The literature on the development and functioning of the
superego is characterized by differences of opinion and emphasis. Freud describes four roots of the superego and defines
three related functions. The superego develops from man's
prehistory, from "the dependent relationships of the ego"
(1923a, p. 48), as "the heir of the Oedipus complex" (p. 36), and
from postoedipal parental substitutes. In regard to its functions, he (1932) states: "We have allotted it the functions of
self-observation, of conscience and of [maintaining] the ideal"
(p. 66).

Freud (1940) considers the superego to have inherited
roots. "The id and the superego have one thing in common:
they both represent the influence of the past" (p. 147). He
(1923a) describes this evolutionary process more specifically:

> The experiences of the ego . . . repeated often enough and with
> sufficient strength in many individuals in successive genera-
> tions, . . . transform themselves, so to say, into experiences of
> the id, the impressions of which are preserved by heredity.
> Thus in the id, which is capable of being inherited, are har-
> boured residues of the existences of countless egos; and when
> the ego forms its super-ego out of the id, it may perhaps only
> be reviving shapes of former egos and be bringing them to
> resurrection [p. 38].

In considering the origins of the superego Freud (1923a)
recognized "two highly important factors, one of a biological
and the other of a historical nature: namely, the lengthy dura-
tion in man of his childhood helplessness and dependence, and
the fact of his Oedipus complex" (p. 35). He further elaborates
the reciprocal and hierarchically organized nature of the
superego:

> Thus we have said repeatedly that the ego is formed to a great
> extent out of identifications which take the place of abandoned
> cathexes by the id; that the *first* of these identifications always
> behave as a special agency in the ego and stand apart from the
> ego in the form of a super-ego, while later on, as it grows
> stronger, the ego may become more resistant to the influences
> of such identifications. The super-ego owes its special position
> in the ego, or in relation to the ego, to a factor which must be
> considered from two sides: *on the one hand it was the first
> identification,* . . . and on the other it is the heir to the Oedipus
> complex [p. 48, emphasis added].

Freud (1923a) has delineated the complexity of the origins
and functions of man's superego in his emphasis on the organizing influence of oedipal factors: "The broad general out-
come of . . . the Oedipus complex [is] the forming of a precipi-
tate in the ego. . . . This modification of the ego . . . confronts
the other contents of the ego as an ego ideal or super-ego. The
super-ego is, however, not simply a residue of the earliest
object-choices of the id; it also represents an energic reaction
formation against these choices" (p. 34). He (1932) describes

the oedipal influences on superego development as "a strong *intensification* of identifications with [the] parents which have probably long been present in [the] ego" (p. 64, emphasis added) and notes the ongoing nature of superego development: "In the course of development the super-ego also takes on the influences of those who have stepped into the place of parents – educators, teachers, people chosen as ideal models. Normally it departs more and more from the original parental figures; it becomes, so to say, more impersonal" (p. 64).

Freud (1923a) emphasizes the drive-controlling, prohibiting function of these oedipal identifications: the "infantile ego fortified itself for the carrying out of the repression by erecting this same obstacle within itself. It borrowed strength so to speak from the father" (p. 34). So armed it could tell itself, "you may not be like this (like your father) – that is, you may not do all that he does; some things are his prerogative" (p. 34). Freud (1932) describes the self-observing function of the superego as "an essential preliminary to the judging activity of conscience" (p. 60).

Freud (1932) also emphasizes a second important superego function: "It is also the vehicle of the ego ideal by which the ego measures itself, which it emulates and whose demand for every greater perfection it strives to fulfill" (pp. 64–66).

Increasing knowledge of development gained from child analysis and infant observation, combined with increasing analytic experience with difficult adult character disorders, has resulted in a greater theoretical emphasis on the development of the representational world, and these factors, in turn, should influence exploration of superego development. In this regard three premises are presented. First, there has been an excessive emphasis on oedipal conflict resolution in various formulations regarding the genesis of the superego. Second, a conglomerate of internalizations that are structured during the preoedipal era in response to preoedipal developmental events and attempted conflict resolutions can be considered a functioning preoedipal superego. Third, there is an important postoedipal superego development that is interminable. The superego, like all structuralizations composed significantly of internalizations, is perennially prone to regressive dedifferentiation and externalization. Most human beings' superegos, to some extent, employ external objects (animate and inanimate) throughout their lives to bolster the superego and the ego in their struggles with repression, conflict resolution, and assimilation.

As Freud has emphasized, the Oedipus complex and its resolution provide an *intensification* that is a profoundly important nodal point in superego development. Such internalizations function to facilitate repression of oedipal longings and serve as additional identifications that contribute to ongoing adaptive development. However, in synchrony with the progressive resolution of the rapprochement struggle, internalizations occur that cluster as introjects and function to provide the subject with a sense of the inner presence of his parents. This presence is the preoedipal superego.

It is of interest that Mahler (et al., 1975) places the "beginnings of superego" (p. 101) at twenty-one months and identifies it as one of three signs of "the growing individuation associated with a general diminishing of the rapprochement struggle" (p. 101). The other two signs are "the development of language [and] symbolic play" (p. 101). The beginnings of superego are defined as "the internalization process, which could be inferred both from acts of identification with the 'good' providing mother and father, and from internalizations of rules and demands" (p. 101).

Freud (1923a) refers to these presences in regard to the origin of the ego ideal: "Behind it there lies hidden an individual's first and most important identification" (p. 31); "by giving permanent expression to the influence of the parents it *perpetuates the existence* of these factors to which it owes its origin" (p. 35, emphasis added). For preoedipal development to proceed, for the subject to achieve the "beginnings of emotional object constancy" (Mahler et al., 1975, p. 109), the illusion of the existence of the parents is perpetuated as an introjected *presence* in the preoedipal superego. This is the original function of the preoedipal superego that "lies hidden behind" its other important functions.

Pertinent literature on superego development clusters into three groups: first, the contributions of Melanie Klein and some of her contemporary colleagues; second, the contributions of more recent ego psychologists; and finally, those of a group of more clinically oriented papers deriving from work with difficult adult character disorders.

Melanie Klein's (1933) pioneering efforts in the analysis of small children (p. 267) have led her to suggest radical theoretical extensions that, in spite of the criticisms they often (I think correctly) evoke, deserve careful consideration. Her shift of emphasis includes three points with current relevance. In 1933, Klein notes that "there could be no doubt a super-ego had been in full operation for some time in my small patients of between two-and-three-quarters and four years of age" (p. 267), and in a later paper, she (1958, p. 239) places these beginnings of the superego more specifically in the sixteenth to eighteenth month of life, which corresponds to the end of the practicing subphase of the separation-individuation process. Important clinical suggestions derive from her temporal shift of emphasis. The early superego is "immeasurably harsher and more cruel than that of the older child or adult, and . . . literally crushe[s] down the feeble ego of the small child" (p. 267). Further, "the child's fear of being devoured, or cut up, or torn to pieces, or its terror of being surrounded and pursued by menacing figures, [is] a regular component of its mental life" (p. 268). From a developmental perspective she notes that "when the genital stage sets in, the child's sadistic instincts have normally been overcome. . . . And as its genital

impulses grow in strength there emerge beneficent and helpful imagos . . . and its super-ego . . . begins to exert a milder
and more persuasive rule. . . . It gradually becomes transformed into conscience in the true sense of the word" (pp.
270–271).

A final point with important theoretical and clinical implications can be drawn from Klein (1933): "It is the excessive
severity and overpowering cruelty of the super-ego, not the
weakness or want of it, as it is usually supposed, which is
responsible for the behavior of asocial and criminal persons"
(p. 270). The statement suggests an active, defensive, identificatory process between these subjects' egos and their introjects. Such introjects are constituted as "primary process
presences" (Schafer,. 1968, p. 82) and should be considered as
preoedipal superegos. Such a dynamically vital orientation
provides a more optimistic theoretical perspective for organizing data of action-prone character disorders than does the
perspective of defective psychic structure being overwhelmed
by drive discharge demands or by the demands of the "pleasure ego" or id.

Melanie Klein has proposed a number of related hypotheses with which most analysts disagree and which may interfere with an appreciation of what I suggest are important aspects of her work. For example, she (1933) proposes that "the
foundation-stone of the development of the superego" (p. 269)
is the conflict between the life and death instincts. Using this
experience-distant theoretical proposition, she derives the
severity and sadism of the preoedipal superego almost entirely from projection and introjection of aggressive drive
cathexes. Rappaport's (1959) reference to some of Klein's
theoretical formulations as "id mythology" (p. 11n.) emphasizes the difficulty that most contemporary analysts have, not
only with Klein's formulation, but also with Freud's (1920)
concept of the death instinct and with theoretical formulations primarily derived from an energic perspective. The role

of the real object in development is minimized in Klein's formulations, as are phallic-oedipal and postoedipal influences on the sadism of the superego. Most difficult for many analysts is her insistence "that the child's Oedipus tendencies, too, begin earlier than has hitherto been thought, i.e., while it is still in the sucking stage" (p. 270n.). Beres's (1958) criticism of Klein is typical:

> Melanie Klein's concept of the central depressive position is based on her theory of early superego formation, early unconscious fantasies, early oedipal conflicts, and the anxieties created by the danger to the ambivalently loved object by the child's aggressive impulses. The point of difference with Melanie Klein would not be in the nature of the process, but in the timing; namely, does internalization and structuralization of superego occur as early as she would indicate? [p. 344].

It is important to note that Beres in 1958 is criticizing Klein's 1933 formulation of the temporal emergence of the superego rather than her own 1958 emendations, which are much closer to Mahler's more recent formulations. The important point is that we may consider that the child is capable of intra- and intersystemic conflict concerning oral and anal sadistic urges without considering that these conflicts have any relationship to those of the phallic-oedipal stage of development.

A number of Melanie Klein's contemporaries show the influence of her important and provocative findings and formulations. In 1926, Jones—in suggesting a more balanced view of superego development, "that the superego . . . combines influences from both the inner and outer world" (p. 305), appreciates the presence function that I am emphasizing: "The image thus incorporated into the (super-)ego serves itself as an object to the libidinal impulses proceeding from the id" (p. 306). "On the one hand [the superego] provides an object for the libidinal impulses of the id when the external object is no longer available, whereas on the other hand it represents the renouncing of incest" (p. 311). Glover (1930), in an important paper, attempts to integrate Klein's work, and that of her coworker Isaacs (1929), with Freud's seminal concept, the superego: "The tendency to scotamatise early stages of Superego formation is a final attempt . . . to screen guilt [and] it would seem that a number of difficult theoretical problems can be resolved provided we do not set out on investigation with too rigid preconceptions as to psychic structure" (p. 11). Glover suggests a "pregenital phase" (p. 8) of superego formation characterized by "unreal distorted objects" (p. 7). In response to Isaacs' paper, he notes that most discussions of superego focus on its *"completion"* rather than on "the *onset* of superego formation" (p. 5). While it is not clear that he agrees with the Kleinian proposition that superego formation begins in the second half of the first year of life, he does consider it functioning by the anal-sadistic stage, which correlates temporally with the rapprochement crisis: "The analysis of obsessional neurotics has shown that it is possible for the ego to achieve a high degree of differentiation (in the Super-ego sense) under the primacy of the anal-sadistic phase, and the presence of distinct obsessional traits in a large number of so-called 'normal' individuals suggests that this early differentiation is a common occurrence" (p. 5).

Isaacs (1929), herself, makes a number of theoretical statements of contemporary relevance. Beginning from the premise that "the structure of the super-ego is 'built up of identifications dating from very different periods and strata in the mental life'" (p. 338), she suggests that "it would seem to be on this background of the sense of being thwarted by the punishing mother for sadistic desires towards her that the more complicated cross-relationships of the Oedipus situation are embroidered" (p. 346). In a similar vein Mahler (et al., 1975) notes that "there is a tendency to underestimate the potentiality of the ego and the precursors of the superego to create intrapsychic conflicts at early levels of development"

(p. 228). Mahler concludes her important book with the thought that "the infantile neurosis becomes manifestly visible at the oedipal period; but it may be shaped by the fate of the rapprochement crisis *that precedes it*" (p. 230).

In the context of his criticism of "Hartmann and his collaborators" (p. 212) and of their explications of aggressive drive development, Schafer (1968) notes that "unlike many present-day theorists, [Freud] viewed the aggressive side of the superego as being altogether primitively fierce and destructive" (p. 211). In this regard, Hartmann, Kris, and Loewenstein (1946), Beres (1958), Sandler (1960), and Hartmann and Loewenstein (1962) place greater emphasis than does Freud on the post-oedipal superego and on the distinction between that integration of the superego and what they refer to as "precursors." This perspective derives from Hartmann's (1939) concept of "autonomy" (pp. 101–108) and may contribute to what Glover (1930) refers to as a "too rigid preconception of psychic structure" (p. 11).

In 1961, at the Edinburgh Congress, Hartmann and Loewenstein (1962), Loewald (1962), and Rosenfeld (1962) participated in a panel on "The Superego and the Ego Ideal." Hartmann and Loewenstein's (1962) report states: "We propose to distinguish clearly such genetic determinants from superego system. . . . The term superego . . . is linked with the resolution of conflicts of the oedipal phase. . . . Its definition rests on its functions (e.g., conscience, self-criticism, the function of holding up ideals)" (p. 43). They, in contrast to Freud, place an excessive emphasis on the "'autonomy' of the superego's functions" (p. 65). In this regard they note: "Freud spoke sometimes of the superego as a differentiated grade 'within the ego.' We consider the superego . . . as a system in its own right" (p. 44). Hartmann and Loewenstein object to the concept of a preoedipal superego because in their view such a concept does not "explain the defensive tendencies or capacities of the ego" (p. 43). Beres (1958) expresses a similar view.

"The early use of reaction formation as a defense against forbidden oral and anal drives is a familiar clinical observation. It
is often an ego response against instinctual danger before the
superego has developed sufficiently to take over this censor-
ing function" (p. 339). I am suggesting that the preoedipal
ego's "use of reaction formation" is overdetermined in response to *both* the strength of the instincts and to the menacing nature of the preoedipal superego.

In a vein similar to Hartmann, Sandler (1960) distinguishes a "preautonomous superego scheme" (p. 152) from a
"the superego proper" (p. 153). Jacobson (1964) also follows
Hartmann and Loewenstein's (1962) perspective and conceives of "early precursors" (p. 93) of the superego leading to a
"new functional system" (p. 89), the superego proper, toward
the end of the oedipal phase. In that regard she considers "the
preoedipal ego ideal as but one among many superego precursors" (p. 123). Her descriptions (see especially pp. 124–125) of
the development of these precursors and their relationship to
the vicissitudes of aggressive drive development are exten-
sive and of significant heuristic value, as are her elaborations
of superego development in latency and adolescence. In contrast to the perspective of this chapter, which suggests that
superego development in many individuals is an interminable
lifelong process, Jacobson believes that "the *final* maturation
of . . . the superego sets in only after the tempest of instinctual conflicts during adolescence has subsided" (p. 130, emphasis added). In contrast Schafer (1968) suggests that
"superego development has already gone through some of its
development before the period during which the oedipal crisis
takes place. . . . Self observation, . . . notions of right and
wrong, or good and bad, do not seem to come into being only
during or after superego crystallization. The insistence that
they can only come into existence that late in development is a
residual of the early days of structural psychology" (p. 105).

Annie Reich (1954), Piers and Singer (1953), Loewald

(1962), and Lampl–de Groot (1962) differ from Hartmann in distinguishing between the oedipal superego and a preoedipal ego ideal. Reich notes that "the superego is a complex structure" (p. 219). In regard to this complexity, she suggests that even the prohibiting functions are overdetermined: "The instinct-restricting identifications, in their task of restricting incestuous genitality, become fused with earlier ones directed against pregenital indulgence" (p. 219). Lampl–de Groot (1962) stresses the preoedipal roots of the ego ideal and emphasizes that it is "essentially a *need-satisfying agency*" (p. 99) "which serves to provide pleasure and undo pain, caused by frustration" (p. 96). In emphasizing what Freud had not, Schafer in his "The Loving and Beloved Superego in Freud's Structural Theory," similarly stresses, from a predominantly oedipal perspective, the need-satisfying aspects of the superego.

The study of the development of the superego has facilitated and been complemented by an inquiry into and a clarification of the nature of processes of incorporation, introjection, internalization, and identification. In that regard, the contributions of Hartmann (1950a), Hartmann and Loewenstein (1962), Sandler (1960), and Schafer (1968) are noteworthy. In a related vein Weissman (1954), in an important but infrequently quoted paper, elaborates Glover's (1930) concept of a pregenital superego in a manner that presages the emphasis of this chapter. Much as Glover has been influenced by Klein's child-analytic data, so too has Weissman been influenced by Fraiberg's (1952) report of a "two-and-a-half-year-old child with many compulsive symptoms" (p. 537).

Weissman suggests that "the fundamental process in superego formation . . . is the introjection of the parental object" (p. 540). He distinguishes and describes an "archaic superego": "The function of the archaic superego is to provide the ego of the infant with a means of sharing the power of its parents and their protection against its instinctual prephallic demands. The function of the genital superego is to bring about the resolution of the Oedipus complex" (p. 531). He notes that "in the archaic superego the aggressive energy attached to the 'prohibiting' introject is least neutralized and more closely approximates instinctual qualities" (p. 531). To emphasize its relationship to introjects and to distinguish it from the "genital" or "mature superego" (p. 531), Weissman suggests that the archaic superego be designated the "introego" (p. 540).

From a similar perspective, Sandler (1960) elaborates Anna Freud's (1936) concept and notes that "we can replace the notion of superego identification with that of *identification with the introject*" (p. 155). In this regard Schafer's (1968) book makes a significant contribution toward the understanding, enlivening, and enriching of the psychoanalytic concepts subsumed under the rubric of processes of internalization. Of an introject: "Its seemingly *independent* ability to influence the subject is its outstanding experiential quality" (p. 83). He proceeds to note that some primary-process presences "are structured as introjects, that is, they are enduring organizations whose rates of changes are slow or negligible, . . . yet they cannot be structures in the same sense that id, ego, and superego are structures for they are not motivational and regulatory organizations" (pp. 130–131). As opposed to the latter part of this statement, and in agreement with Glover's concept of a "pregenital superego" and Weissman's concept of "introego" and in elaboration of Anna Freud's (1936) and Sandler's (1960) concept of "identification with the introject," I am emphasizing that introjects are profoundly motivational – that narcissistic, masochistic, sadistic, and self-destructive identifications of the ego are motivated, in part, by the presence of introjects that comprise the preoedipal superego. These identifications significantly contribute to the character organizations of subjects who prove most difficult to help with psychoanalytic treatment.

Corresponding to the theoretical interest in superego development there have appeared a series of more clinically oriented papers on masochism and negative therapeutic reaction. Although Melanie Klein is only rarely quoted in these papers, as Sandler (1960) notes, "there can be little doubt that the controversial propositions of Melanie Klein regarding superego development have stimulated others to direct more attention to superego precursors in the preoedipal phase" (p. 142). This is particularly true in discussions of "difficult patients who tend to be refractionary to psychoanalytic treatment... many of whom have the propensity to be deeply attached to pain" (Valenstein, 1973, p. 365).

Bergler has written a series of papers and books on masochism. In his *Curable and Incurable Neurotics*, he elaborates a view of development and pathogenesis that is more extreme but strikingly similar to Melanie Klein's. In this fascinating and useful work, he places "the origin of guilt" (p. 32), the oedipal phase, and superego development in the first two years of life:

> The combination of fear and ambivalence in the preoedipal levels makes the child's situation unbearably difficult, and it is this that pushes him, at the age of one and a half or two, into the oedipal phase [p. 43].

Further:

> In his frantic effort to hold onto vestiges of his most cherished infantile fantasy – omnipotence, megalomania, autarchy – the child of two or two-and-a-half... identifies with the prohibitions handed down by his mother and father. He thus substitutes an *inner* prohibition for the barrage of *external* prohibitions [p. 32].

This results in the formation of the superego whose "technique is torture for torture's sake" (p. 34).

Bergler's suggestions as to the timing of the formation of the superego correspond to Melanie Klein's later views and Mahler's more recent suggestions. For Bergler, psychic masochism and superego formation are the narcissistic solutions of the toddler struggling to maintain the vestiges of his "original narcissistic perfection." This formulation is strikingly similar to Freud's (1914, p. 94) original conception of the formation of the ego ideal. With a view almost identical to Kohut's (1977) recent conception of oedipal issues as "disintegration products" (p. 262) of struggles of the self, Bergler notes that "the oedipal phase is but a 'rescue station from unbearable pre-oedipal fears'" (p. 44). "The deeper layers are dynamically more decisive than the superficial ones, especially since the more superficial only express in a new language the contents of the deeper layers" (p. 56). Rosenfeld (1962), from a Kleinian perspective, has expressed a similar view: "The analysis of the later superego is often dynamically of secondary importance because it has mainly a defensive function against the anxieties of the early superego" (p. 261).

Freud, Melanie Klein, and Bergler emphasize the death instinct and the vicissitudes of aggressive drive cathexis in the genesis of masochism. Berliner (1958), Loewenstein (1957), and Valenstein (1973) emphasize parental aggression in the genesis of masochism, negative therapeutic reaction, and certain difficult patients' attachment to pain. I would also add that representations of these real sadistic objects are internalized as introjects whose *presence* constitutes a fundamental cornerstone of these subjects' superegos. Berliner (1958) notes: "Still in historic time – it was customary and legally permitted to kill unwanted children" (p. 42). And: "The ill-treating parent does not belong to the dim prehistoric past" (p. 43). He emphasizes "that the introjection of another person's sadism is the essential pattern in masochism" (p. 51). Loewenstein (1957) describes "seduction of the aggressor" as ubiquitous behavior that aids children in assimilating their parents' aggression toward them and which "already contains elements of future masochistic behavior" (p. 215). Valenstein (1973) notes that "the core of the negative therapeutic reaction in these instances comes from the patients' attachment to pain" (p. 366). "Attachment to pain signifies an original attachment to painfully perceived objects and inconstant objects at that. . . . The painful affects are then held to both as a defense and as an instinctually charged concomitant of object experience" (p. 389).

The premises of this chapter are derived from a psychoanalytic, developmental perspective that integrates data from all levels of development and judges the relative importance of particular influences on individual analysands. There has been a tendency toward a polarizing either/or perspective in considering the relative importance of preoedipal versus oedipal issues in general and in the genesis of the superego in particular. Hartmann and his collaborators stress the latter while Melanie Klein, Rosenfeld, and Bergler insist on the former. I (1979b) have previously stressed the importance of "*both*" (p. 192) factors in the genesis of narcissistic personality disorders and am here stressing both factors in the genesis of the superego. Freud (1932) emphasizes that "pathology, by making things larger and coarser can draw attention to normal conditions which would otherwise have escaped us" (p. 58). The difficult patients described by Valenstein (1973) draw our attention to the foundations of the superego. These patients are not motivated solely by an unconscious need for punishment derived from a sense of oedipal guilt. Rather they are significantly motivated to establish an object relationship with a pain-rendering object who is chosen because of its similarity to the pain rendering presence structured as introject in their preoedipal superego. In healthier patients, such a preoedipal factor may be fused with and influence a subject's oedipal conflicts and be woven into the fabric of his oedipal guilt. I believe Freud (1923a) is alluding to this complexity when he notes that "a sense of guilt. . . is often the sole remaining trace of the abandoned love-relation" (p. 50n.).

Both Jones and Glover emphasize the complexity of the

superego's genesis and functioning. Jones (1926) states that "the concept of the superego is a nodal point where we may expect all the obscure problems of the Oedipus complex and narcissism on the one hand, and hate and sadism on the other to meet" (p. 304). And Glover (1930) suggests that "we may say . . . that the Super-Ego develops simultaneously with the ego, a differentiation in function becoming more obvious with each stage of development, or . . . that both the Super-Ego and Ego are struck out of a primitive pleasure Ego, itself derived from the Id, or . . . [that] the Super-Ego is first differentiated from the primitive pleasure Ego, the Real-Ego being . . . an important byproduct of conflict between the Super-Ego and the Primitive Pleasure Ego" (p. 6).

According to Freud, the preoedipal superego develops from man's biological helplessness and the resulting prolonged dependency and immaturity of the ego. Man is unable to live without some sense of his parent's presence. Further, optimal development cannot proceed without the presence of respectable and related parental objects. He (1914) emphasizes man's insatiability in his formulation of the genesis of the ego ideal: "Man is incapable of giving up a satisfaction he once enjoyed" (p. 94). Lampl–de Groot (1962) emphasizes this *"need satisfying"* function which Freud (1923a) expresses in a more global context: "The super-ego fulfills the . . . function of protecting and saving" (p. 58).

Loewald (1962) anticipates an emphasis of this chapter in his description of "the ego's function of . . . *creating and recreating presence* as the temporal aspect of its synthetic or organizing function" (p. 264, emphasis added).

The superego by virtue of its *presence* within the preoedipal child provides illusions of security and of the possibility of gratification. This is its fundamental function. As development proceeds, other contents and more specific functions are elaborated that contribute to oedipal conflict resolution and facilitate progressive adaptation. By creating the illusion of inner safety and love these presences protect the subject from more than the dangers of external reality. They contribute to the diminution, regulation, and assimilation of the subject's cannibalistic, anal-sadistic, phallic-oedipal, and postoedipal murderous rage that is evoked by the privations (Isaacs, 1929) inevitably experienced, and the frustrations derived from, involvement with the real parental objects.

The primary process elaboration of the subject's aggressive drive endowment is influenced by the subject's "basic core" (Weil, 1970) and by the real quality of the parental objects. These factors influence contents associated with the introjected parental presences as well as with the ego's defensive identificatory responses to these introjections. Narcissistic, masochistic, and sadistic ego attributes derive, in part, in defensive response to the introject.

These identifications of the ego contribute to the subject's defensive avoidance of experiences of disappointment, rage, and anxiety. In addition they contribute to the longed for sense of harmony between the subject and his preoedipal superego.

From a developmental perspective, I am criticizing Hartmann's emphasis on the autonomy of the superego's conscience function. His perspective stresses a relatively mature postoedipal integration of the superego that is characterized by its impersonality, stability of function, and guilt as its signal affect and that is also associated with the attainment of object constancy. There has been a tendency to idealize this structuralization and the concept of normality that derives from it. I am emphasizing the variability of superego integration in relationship to conflict. The superego may function as a depersonified structure, however, it is always vulnerable to regressive dedifferentiation to its oedipal and preoedipal integrations that are personified, menacing, and sadistic. In a similar vein, Mahler's elaboration of object constancy is a relative one. Human beings are "on the way to" object constancy.

Many adults who appear "fully separated and individuated" are organized in relationship to unconscious fantasied presences in their institutional and societal affiliations. Finally, while guilt is the signal affect of the postoedipal superego, castration anxiety, panic, terror, and a panoply of other anxieties (annihilation) are the signal affects of the oedipal and preoedipal integrations of the superego.

Optimal personality development in general and superego development in particular are dependent upon and facilitated by the real external presence of respected and related parents through adolescence – for many, perhaps even into adulthood. It is true that related objects can serve as surrogates for disappointing, unrelated, inconsistent, or even absent or dead parents. However, the identifications with these surrogates, although salutary, defend, in part, against mourning the parental object. These occasionally life-saving compensatory identifications defend against the "assimilation" (Waelder, 1936, p. 48) by the ego of the true nature of the parental object. The dormant parental images are revivified in the transference where mourning, that was not possible in childhood (Wolfenstein, 1966, 1969), may occur.

Meiss (1952), in a fascinating report of the analysis of a child in oedipal phase development whose father had died, emphasizes the ongoing necessity for the presence of a respectable parental object:

> Since there was no actual father present to reassure the child that wishes are not the same as deeds, or to continue giving and evoking affection, his fearsome image could not be tested against reality. Through the analysis this terrifying father image was replaced by a just but kindly one. . . . He re-enacted and further developed his early relationship to his father by manifesting hostility toward the analyst's husband and at the same time emulating him [p. 228].

Hartmann, Kris, and Loewenstein (1946) allude to the ongoing nature of superego development. They note "that the potentialities of its transformation throughout latency and adolescence have for some time been underrated in psychoanalytic writings" (p. 34). Blos (1962), in his description of "mourning" (p. 187) as an important aspect of adolescence, contributes to our understanding of superego development during that epoch. It is typical for adolescents to seek idealized surrogates to defend against mourning and for their analytic processes to be characterized by such cathectic vicissitudes (A. Freud, 1958). These phenomena highlight the ongoing search for external presences to assuage the pain of mourning the real nature of the adolescent's inner presence.

Many midlife adults confront contemporary analysts with problems that reflect the ongoing nature of superego development, its dependence on external presences, and the influence of the values and ideals of a society on one's larger sense of presence. In a related vein many contemporary midlife adults have lived in synchrony with superegos that are the structured repositories of the values and ideals of their parents. These values and ideals are no longer sufficiently enforced by the external presences of the extended nuclear family or the institution of religion. As many midlife adults confront the perception of the depressing limits of their lives, they are simultaneously "permitted and encouraged" by newer values in their society that prize activity, sensuality, and possessions as "antidepressants." These common events emphasize the importance of an external idealizable presence in reenforcing and supporting the conscience function of the adult superego. Perhaps it is only a most unusual individual whose superego functions without any support from others who share his values. The difficult question is raised as to what influence the analyst's values have on analytic process. In this regard Strachey (1934) describes "the analyst as auxiliary super-ego" (p. 139) and Loewald (1962) suggests that "patients re-externalize aspects of their superego by projecting them onto the analyst and internalize aspects of . . . the analyst's relationship with the patient" (p. 267). In this sense Loewald's suggestion extends Strachey's (1934) concept of a "mutative" (p. 143) interpretation. Strachey views the analyst as a new, "benign" (p. 138) object whose internalization provides a mutative presence for the "vicious" internalizations that comprise the subject's superego.

The analytic relationship is a unique growth-promoting experience for some midlife adults. An analysand's relatedness may be strengthened, in part, by an identification with his analyst's value of listening and understanding another person based on a respect for his autonomy, rather than for his narcissistic or need-satisfying potential. This may be a particularly important new experience for some successful people in our technological era who view their mates as animate possessions to complement and facilitate their careers. New mutative identifications may occur throughout life with one's family, friends, colleagues, and superiors. However, the regression intrinsic to an analytic experience renders such mutative processes more likely if not inevitable. Profound disappointment in one's parents may delay and distort the development of aspects of an analysand's psychic structure. However, such traumatic formative experiences may also contribute to a subject's potential availability to new identificatory experiences. In addition, these new experiences stand in stark contrast to traumatic formative experiences. The contrast facilitates associations and the interpretation of distortions experienced in the transference and contributes to the acquisition of insight that facilitates mourning and progressive individuation.

Freud (1926) asks a question of central relevance to understanding the mode of therapeutic action of the analysis of preoedipal fixations in superego development: "When does separation from an object produce anxiety, . . . mourning . . . or maybe, only pain?" (p. 169).

I am suggesting that for these analysands to tolerate the pain associated with mourning the presences that comprise their preoedipal superegos, they require the "holding" presence of another person. This is explicit in Modell's (1976) appli-

cation of Winnicott's (1960) concept of the holding environment as well as in the mourning rituals of most societies. A
holding environment alone provides a supportive psychotherapy. Its interdigitation with interpretation helps create an
analytic experience that may facilitate ego development and
progressive individuation. Such a developmental process can
slowly diminish the requirement to be "held."

The advantage of the concept of a preoedipal superego is
that it renders the concepts superego and intersystemic conflict more useful in organizing clinical data derived from work
with "difficult" character disorders. Their character organizations are more felicitously appreciated when viewed from a
developmental perspective and emphasis. This emphasis
stresses the characteristics of variability of integration at moments in time, of progressive and regressive shifts, and of
both preoedipal and oedipal nodal points as organizers of
character development and symptomatology. In addition, a
developmental perspective emphasizes that traumatic events
at any stage of development can serve as nodal points which
may engender regressive dedifferentiation of superego structuralizations with a resultant reorganization at oedipal or preoedipal levels of integration.

Freud (1937) explains some of these subjects' difficulties as
deriving from an inherited characteristic of their basic cores:
their "adhesiveness of the libido" (p. 241) and its "psychical
inertia" (p. 242). However, his explication of "adhesiveness of
the libido" suggests that from an energic perspective, he may
be organizing clinical data deriving from these subjects' intense attachment to their preoedipal superegos: "The process
which the treatment sets in motion in them is so much slower
than in other people because, apparently, they cannot make
up their minds to detach libidinal cathexes from one object
and displace them onto another" (p. 241).

Sicker character disorders (narcissistic personality disorders, borderline personality organizations, masochistic

characters, those attached to pain, acting-out characters, etc.) seem to "hold" on to their illnesses. This derives, in part, from their tenacious investment in maintaining a relationship between themselves and the primary process presences structured as introjects in the foundations of their preoedipal superegos.

It is often suggested that certain character disorders cannot experience guilt because their superegos have lacunae or are defective. While this is undoubtedly true of some people, I have seen a number of narcissistic personality disorders who can experience guilt but whose conscience function lacks an *enforcing presence*. Such subjects' superegos are fixated, in part, at the oedipal level. Freud (1932) refers to subjects such as these when he suggests "that the superego is stunted in its strength . . . if the surmounting of the Oedipus complex is only incompletely successful" (p. 64). Their superegos cannot, to paraphrase Freud (1923a), "borrow the strength of their fathers" (p. 34) because their fathers are perceived to be disappointing.

Their parents are truly weak and not admirable. Often they lack integrity and have problems in their own superego development that lead them to be perceived as saying "Do as I say, not as I do." Other parents may have been absent, ill, or may have died during their children's development. Their behavior in and out of the transference, is often, in part, a provocative and defiant attempt to provoke a respectable, idealizable, related object to become an enforcing parental presence. Analytic mourning facilitates reexperiencing traumatic disappointment in the parents. The resulting ego development helps the subject to suppress wishes and accept limits rather than affording a repair of the superego's capacity to enforce and support repression and other unconscious defensive processes. This perspective is suggested in Freud's (1932) statement that the intention of psychoanalysis is "to strengthen the ego, to make it more independent of the super-ego" (p. 80).

# CHAPTER 4

# Trauma and the Repetition Compulsion

*Had he stayed with the initial formulation the outline*
*of a truly dynamic ego psychology might have evolved*
*from* Beyond the Pleasure Principle.

George Klein, *Psychoanalytic Theory*

In a series of important papers written during the second decade of this century, Freud struggles to understand and conceptualize man's penchant for self-involvement and self-destructiveness. In these papers, written when Freud's theoretical constructs were in a state of transition, he discusses issues from an ego-psychological perspective without the organizing framework of a refined structural hypothesis. The considerations of narcissism (1914), depression (1917a), and sadomasochism (1905, 1915) are written within the framework of the dual-instinct theory of libido and the self-preservative instinct, with little emphasis given to "non-erotic" (Freud, 1930, p. 120) aggression. These efforts leave Freud unsatisfied in his understanding of man's pursuit of experiences seeming to repeat events that offer no apparent pleasure and that are often painful and self-destructive. His dissatisfaction results in the brilliant and highly speculative *Beyond the Pleasure Principle*. In this paper Freud proposes hypotheses in order to explain "ultimate things, the great problems of science and life" (p. 59). Pursuant to this end he resorts to an experience-distant elaboration of instinct theory,

the death instinct, and, at times, relies heavily on explanations elaborated in energic terminology.

The enigmatic clinical data derived from experiences
"beyond the pleasure principle" can be more felicitously
understood and worked with if they are described in the less
experience-distant theoretical terms and concepts of modern
ego psychology. From an ego-psychological perspective,
trauma is defined as any perception (internal or external) the
ego is unable to assimilate by any of its integrative operations.
This results in affective disorganization that may motivate
assimilative attempts at repetition and a variety of other
defensive responses including narcissistic, sadistic, and masochistic identifications.

Freud (1920) describes five categories of human experience in which people pursue pain rather than immediate gratification: (1) behavior organized under the aegis of the "reality
principle" (p. 10), (2) experiences of "conflict" (pp. 10–11),
(3) repetitions in the traumatic neuroses (pp. 13–14), (4) repetitions in children's play (pp. 15–16), and, most important,
(5) "the compulsion to repeat" (p. 20).

Freud observes his one-and-one-half-year-old nephew's
play in response to his mother's departure and notes:

> The child cannot possibly have felt his mother's departure as
> something agreeable or even indifferent. How then does his
> repetition of this distressing experience as a game fit in with
> the pleasure principle? . . . The child turned his experience into
> a game from another motive. At the onset he was in a *passive*
> situation – he was overpowered by the experience; but, by
> repeating it, unpleasurable though it was, as a game, he took
> on an *active* part. . . . We are therefore left in doubt as to
> whether the impulse to work over in the mind some over-
> powering experience *so as to make oneself master of it* can find
> expression as a primary event, and independent of the pleas-
> ure principle. For in the case we have been discussing, the
> child may, after all, only have been able to repeat his unpleas-

ant experience in play because the repetition carried along with it a yield of pleasure of another sort but none the less a direct one [p. 16, emphasis added].

Freud's second theory of anxiety derives from an ego-psychological elaboration of his clinical, rather than energic, conceptualization of trauma. Signals of anxiety are derived from the ego's assimilation and organization of traumatic experiences in the service of adaptation. Freud (1926) suggests that "anxiety is therefore on the one hand an expectation of trauma, and on the other a repetition of it in a mitigated form" (p. 166). "The ego, which experienced the trauma passively, now repeats it actively in a weakened version, in the hope of being able itself to direct its course" (p. 167).

As Freud pursues and deepens his exposition of the compulsion to repeat in *Beyond the Pleasure Principle*, his constructions become progressively more distant from observable data: "The compulsion to repeat . . . recalls from the past experiences which include no possibility of pleasure, and which can never, even long ago, have brought satisfaction" (p. 20). He notes that "no lesson has been learnt from the old experience of these activities having led instead only to unpleasure" (p. 21) and concludes that "enough is left unexplained to justify the hypothesis of a compulsion to repeat — something that seems more primitive, more elementary, *more instinctual* than the pleasure principle which it over-rides" (p. 23, emphasis added).

To further elucidate his understanding of the compulsion to repeat, Freud (1920) describes and defines the stimulus barrier as a "protective shield" (p. 27) against trauma. Such concepts are defined in an adaptational context and in a mechanistic neurophysiologic metaphor reminiscent of *The Project* and the experience-distant aspects of Chapter 7 of *The Interpretation of Dreams*. "Protection against stimuli is an almost more important function for the living organism than reception of stimuli. The protective shield . . . must

above all endeavor to preserve the special modes of transformation of energy operating in it against the effects threatened by the enormous energies at work in the external world"
(1920, p. 27). He characterizes "as 'traumatic' any excitations
from outside which are powerful enough to break through the
protective shield. . . . The concept of trauma necessarily implies a connection of this kind with a breach in an otherwise
efficacious barrier against stimuli" (p. 29). Although one or-
dinarily thinks of trauma as deriving from "outside," it is
fascinating to note that Freud emphasizes the importance of
internally derived trauma and in that context describes the
defense mechanism of projection: "The fact that the cortical
layer which receives stimuli is without any protective shield
against excitations from within must have as its result that
these latter transmissions of stimulus have a preponderance
in economic importance and often occasion economic disturbances comparable with traumatic neuroses" (p. 34). On "the
origin of *projection*": "A particular way is adopted of dealing
with any internal excitations which produce too great an increase of unpleasure: there is a tendency to treat them as
though they were acting, not from the inside, but from the outside, so that it may be possible to bring the shield against stimuli into operation as a means of defense against them" (p. 29).

   In his discussion of traumatic neuroses, Freud (1920) notes
that "the wish-fulfilling function of dreaming [in traumatic
neurosis is] divested from its purpose" (p. 13). In a fascinating
revision of this sentence in 1921, he adds "or we may be driven
to reflect on the mysterious masochistic trends of the ego"
(pp. 13–14). He explains these dreams as reflecting the "original function" (p. 33) of dreams that attends "to the psychical
binding of traumatic impressions" (p. 33) and proposes that
the dreams of the "traumatic neuroses, or the dreams during
psychoanalysis which bring to memory the psychical traumas
of childhood" (p. 32) derive from the "original function" of the
dreamwork which is analogous to the compulsion to repeat. I

will explore some of the implications of the "original function" of the dream in Chapter 7.

Within an energic metaphor, Freud creates an elaboration of his instinct theory, the death instinct, to explain the compulsion to repeat. Suggesting that the energy of the sun evoked life in inorganic substance, he posits the compulsion to repeat as derived from an inherent quality of organic matter to be compelled to return to its original inorganic state, "to die in its own fashion" (p. 39). He proposes that "the ego instincts [or death instincts] arise from the coming to life of inanimate matter and seek to restore the inanimate state" (p. 44).

Freud's courage as a pioneer and his brilliance as a clinician and theoretician are universally admired. In *Beyond the Pleasure Principle,* he exhibits a freedom for creative speculation combined with a self-critical awareness of the potential limits and partially irrational roots of such hypotheses. This combination of character traits has provided contemporary and future analysts with a legacy within which to elaborate his contribution and from which to embark on more original endeavors. "Unfortunately, however, people are seldom impartial where ultimate things, the great problems of science and life, are concerned. Each of us is governed in such cases by deep internal prejudices, into whose hands our speculations unwittingly plays" (p. 59). Of his "far-fetched speculations" (p. 24) he notes: "I do not know how far I believe in them. . . . [They] cannot lay claim to the same degree of certainty as . . . the extension of the concept of sexuality and the hypothesis of narcissism. These two innovations were a direct translation of observation into theory" (p. 59).

In *The Ego and the Id* Freud embarks on a "further development of some trains of thought which I opened up in *Beyond the Pleasure Principle*" (1923a, p. 12). He conceives of the former work as "stand[ing] closer to psycho-analysis. . . . It is more in the nature of synthesis than of a speculation" (p. 12). From the less experience-distant vantage point of the structural hypothesis, Freud again expresses his doubts about his eros-thanatos hypothesis: "There is . . . no doubt about the pleasure principle, . . . but the distinction between two classes of instincts does not seem sufficiently assured and it is possible that facts of clinical analysis may be found which will do away with its pretention" (p. 42). By 1930, however, Freud has become convinced of "the ubiquity of non-erotic aggressivity and destructiveness" (p. 120), but believes their source inextricably derived from his death instinct hypothesis. Of the latter, he notes, "To begin with [i.e., in 1920] it was only tentatively that I put forward the views I have developed here, but in the course of time they have gained such a hold upon me that I can no longer think in any other way" (p. 119).

Pioneering analysts such as Alexander (1929), Melanie Klein (1933), and Bergler (1961) accept the hypothesis of the death instinct. Heilbrunn, in a fascinating article "Biologic Correlates of Psychoanalytic Concepts," suggests that

> the recent discovery of a substance, somewhat dramatically introduced as "death hormone" (Bylinsky, 1976) may vindicate Freud and verify once again his predictive genius. . . . Denkla (1975, 1977) holds that the life span of mammals is regulated by a biological clock which acts on endocrine glands to produce the failure of the immune and circulatory systems. The hypothalamic-pituitary axis and the pituitary factor provide the mechanism by which the organism prepares and controls its own demise [1979, p. 610].

However, most analysts would agree with Arlow's (1956) opinion concerning the concept of the death instinct. He suggests that "such biological speculations are undesirable in the context of clinical discussions, since they involve extrapolations which are incapable of confirmation or contradiction in this setting" (p. 526).

I (1980b) have previously suggested that "metaphors such as the 'death instinct'. . . were coined to 'explain' what Freud could not explain with constructs that were closer to clinical experience. Theoretical explanations steeped in biology are narcissistically invested and help the analyst live more comfortably with the limits of his psychological understanding" (p. 389).

Freud (1920) proposes an adaptational and an instinctual explanation for behavior "beyond the pleasure principle." As George Klein (1976) suggests: "The antimony Freud saw between his alternative explanations is more apparent than real" (p. 263). A solely adaptational explanation leaves one question unanswered: Why the compulsive repetition? Why doesn't the "reality-ego" learn from experience? No fully satisfactory adaptational explanation being available to him, Freud resorts to biological hypotheses explaining the "compulsion to repeat as more instinctual than the pleasure principle which it over-rides" (p. 23). This emphasis not only carries the disadvantages of being incapable of testing in the clinical setting, but, by linking aggression to an experience-distant theoretical construct like the death instinct, its molecular determinism can also serve as a subtle resistance against accepting full responsibility for one's pleasure in hurting others and oneself. Man must ultimately assimilate his murderous rage and his perceptions of the murderous rage of his loved ones. He must be able to say: "At moments I have felt or feel like killing my mother, father, wife, children, and myself, and they have felt like killing me." The concept of the death instinct mitigates a fuller appreciation of the adaptive significance of aggression and activity.

Freud (1920) suggests that the ego instincts "exercise a pressure toward death; . . . predicate a conservative, or rather retrograde, character corresponding to a compulsion to repeat; . . . and seek to restore the inanimate state" (p. 44). The important word is "inanimate." If the word *inanimate* is changed to "quiescent" or "pleasant," then the repetition compulsion can be understood to derive from the human infant's desire for pleasure. Stage-four sleep could serve as a prototype for such quiescence. This suggests, as infant observation implies, that the infant either is born with or very early acquires a limited capacity for experiencing itself and for actively seeking to maintain a satisfied state. Difficulties arise from the infant's limited capacities for achieving that goal. External traumas become internal traumas via processes of internalization. Maladaptive responses to these traumatic experiences and their representations result in psychopathology.

Freud (1914), in his conception of the development of the ego ideal, views man as insatiable: "Man has here again shown himself as incapable of giving up a satisfaction he had once enjoyed. He is not willing to forgo the narcissistic perfection of his childhood" (p. 94). In *The Ego and the Id* Freud describes identification (pp. 28–29) as a fundamental process of ego development and links it to the ubiquity of man's insatiability: "It may be that this identification is the sole condition under which the id can give up its objects" (p. 29).

In developing his second theory of anxiety, Freud (1926) defines trauma as the passive experience of helplessness. This is his prototype. The primal traumas, and therefore the primal danger situations, are derived from preverbal memory traces of experiences of mounting tension that have never become conscious in the true sense and are in a state of primary repression. The infantile ego's experience of these primal traumas is influenced by its "basic core" (Weil, 1970) and by the quality of its caretaking environment.

Freud links the compulsion to repeat to an instinctually derived, preprogrammed, elemental, molecular compulsion to return to a simpler form of inorganic organization. In his seminal paper on overdetermination, Waelder (1936) considers the compulsion to repeat as one of four factors – along with the id, the superego, and external world – that the ego in its adaptational struggle strives to assimilate. I am suggesting that the ego in Waelder's formulation is analogous to Freud's (1911a) "reality ego" (p. 224). Waelder observes that "it is customary in psychoanalysis to consider the compulsion to repeat as part of the id (its lowermost layer)" (p. 47). Aware of the theoretical dilemma, he adds that although it is not his intention "to give a more far-reaching opinion concerning the status of the compulsion to repeat, . . . it nevertheless seems to us propitious to distinguish between the claims of those impulses which require concrete gratification and the demands of the tendencies to repeat and continue former actions, even those which are unpleasant" (p. 47).

The compulsion to repeat can be understood as a more immature organization of the ego that reflcts and repeats "specific methods. . . of problem solving" (Waelder, 1936, p. 55) deriving from its attempts to organize and assimilate primal and other traumatic experiences. These methods are often maladaptive and responsible for considerable suffering. This immature ego organization, which strives to undo the passively experienced trauma, is associated with such defenses as denial, projection, externalization, and a panoply of defensive identifications. The compulsion to repeat derives, in part, from the fact that the memory of a past traumatic experience festers like an insulting foreign body whose presence threatens the integrity of the narcissistically invested self-representation-as-agent. That integration of the self-representation strives for control of the executive functions of the ego in an effort to erase the memory of the past traumatic experience by recreating and mastering it in the present. Repetition is more commonly associated with moments of ego regression such as occur during sleep. At such times, the efforts of the narcissistically invested self-representation-as-agent may dominate the dreamwork and reflect a derivative of its "original function." In addition, the reality testing and judgment functions associated with this immature ego organization are often impaired. Nevertheless even during sleep the self-representation-as-agent that is organized in response to the reality principle, what Freud referred to as the "reality

ego," struggles to assimilate this immature ego organization
that is compelled to recreate facsimilies of past traumatic experiences. A subject's telling himself in a dream that "this is only a
dream" reflects more than secondary revision: it represents, in
addition, the "reality ego's" ongoing efforts at assimilation.

The question of when in the maturing infant's development the compulsion to repeat appears may be answered with
greater certainty as psychoanalytic theory finds increased synchrony with the rapidly developing data of infant observation.
Still, it is important to note that an infant with an impaired
basic core or an infant who is profoundly out of synchrony
with the expectations and capacities of its caretaking environment is more likely to develop a fixation on modes of problem
solving related to attempts at active reversal of traumatic experience. In this regard, Bellak and Meyers (1975), in their
paper on analyzability, suggest that "patients with . . . minimal brain dysfunction" (p. 425) may have difficulty sorting
"out excessive stimulation by specifically synthesizing the
various stimuli to arrive at an understanding of the specific
situation" (pp. 424–425). Such patients, who as adults exhibit
disorders in their "synthetic integrative function" (p.424),
may as infants have been more likely to experience mounting
tensions and their object worlds as traumatic.

In this chapter, the aggressive instinct is considered a biologic source of emotional energy organized by the immature
ego to become a drive in the service of dealing adaptively with
a frustrating environment. The roots of masochism and
sadism develop early in response to the satisfying and frustrating object. In contrast to George Klein's (1976) view, the
aggressive drive is not conceived of as a "blind drive energy"
(p. 154). In elaboration of the perspective proposed by Hartmann (1950a) and Waelder (1960), the aggressive drive is
conceived of as a biologically derived source of energy that is
organized by an ego and superego composed, in part, of a

variety of self- and object representations. These representations, in a variety of integrations, influence the expression of the subject's rage. The personality organization of the normal or neurotic character has a greater capacity for the internal organization, modulation, and discharge of these drives. Other personality organizations, such as those of the "typical" narcissistic personality disorder, whose superegos are less well integrated offer less opportunity for internal organization of the aggressive drive. They are more prone to experience it in traumatic intensities that result in projection of rage, externalization of superego introjects, and alloplastic discharge of aggressive drive derivatives.

Freud's concepts of ego and ego-ideal formation reflect his intuitive awareness that development is facilitated by and is, in part, an adaptation to separation-individuation, which, in turn, can be understood as a normal developmental "trauma." It is traumatic in that the toddler's immature ego is not equipped to assimilate the narcissistic injuries implicit in the process. Narcissistically invested internalizations attempt to magically and actively undo the experience. This prospective is fundamental to Kohut's (1966) conception of the developments of narcissism, the grandiose self, and the idealizing parent imago. Mahler (1972), striving to understand issues similar to those that preoccupied Freud in 1920, suggests that "one could regard the entire life cycle as constituting . . . an eternal longing for the actual or fantasied 'ideal state of self' with the latter standing for symbiotic fusion with the 'all good' symbiotic mother, who was at one time part of the self in a blissful state of well-being" (p. 338). In discussing the implications of her infant research for an understanding of "borderline mechanisms, which indicate a degree of failure of the synthetic function of the ego" (1971, p. 414), Mahler emphasizes the "optimal emotional availability" (p. 410) of the maternal object during the rapprochement subphase.

Freud (1920) employs Greek and Indian mythology (Plato's

*Symposium* and the *Brihadâranyaka-upanishad*) to support his death instinct hypothesis. In his view, these myths "trace the origin of an instinct to a need to restore an earlier state of things" (p. 57). He notes that Plato describes Zeus cutting "men in two. . . . After the division had been made, 'the two parts of man, each desiring his other half, came together, and threw their arms about one another eager to grow into one'" (pp. 57–58). Freud similarly quotes Yagñavalkya, the Indian philosopher: "We two are thus (each of us) like half a shell. Therefore the void which was there is filled by the wife" (p. 58n.).

In light of the data of infant research and of more recent theoretical formulations concerning the development of the representational world, it is possible to conjecture that these quotes more closely support the constructions of Jacobson (1964) and Mahler. It is possible, if not probable, that had Freud possessed the benefit of these data he might have given greater emphasis to his observations of children's play in his understanding of the genesis of the repetition compulsion.

Freud was aware of all stages of development in his understanding of the human situation. In the midst of his experience-distant speculations on the development of the death instinct and the vicissitudes of processes of binding psychic energies, he (1920) demonstrates a profound awareness of the importance of projection, of the oral phase of development, and even of the processes of separation-individuation: "During the oral stage of the organization of the libido, the act of obtaining erotic mastery over an object coincides with that object's destruction" (p. 54). Despite this awareness, Freud emphasizes the oedipal phase of development and its resolution as the most important nodal point in the genesis of neurosis. He considers its resolution, and the associated progressive development of the superego, as central to the maintenance of object relations and the family, and to the development of civilization. Within this context oral and anal developments are conceived of and emphasized as places (i.e., fixation points) to which a subject's libido may regress in the face of neurotic conflict. In contrast, others have deemphasized regressions of this sort and have described development from a primarily linear perspective. This is particularly true of the Kleinians (M. Klein, 1933; Rosenfeld, 1962), Bergler (1961), and more recently Kohut (1977). These contributors emphasize preoedipal development and the vicissitudes of conflict in that stage of development, as well as the traumatic nature of the primary caretaking environment, as central to their understanding of development in general and the genesis of serious character pathology in particular. For these colleagues, oedipal development is simply a reworking of past conflicts in somewhat disguised form (Rosenfeld, 1962, pp. 258–261) or merely a "disintegration product" (Kohut, 1977, p. 262) of vicissitudes of the cohesion of the self. Even Mahler (et al., 1975) ends her important book with a similar emphasis: "The infantile neurosis becomes manifestly visible at the oedipal period; but it may be shaped by the fate of the rapprochement crisis *that precedes it*" (p. 230).

The tendency to view development as linear or to organize data from an either/or perspective does not satisfy the complexity of the data of human experience. Psychoanalysis does not, at the present time, possess a theoretical framework for conceptualizing the influence of preoedipal development on later experiences and, more importantly, for understanding the reverberating influences of later developmental events in reworking and reorganizing the results of earlier experiences. Perhaps the development of a more adequate psychoanalytic theory of cognitive development, and of symbolization in particular, may contribute a clarification of these issues.

Nevertheless it is important to emphasize that traumatic events at the oedipal and postoedipal stages of development can revivify and reorganize preoedipal traumatic fixations that were minimal and reasonably well assimilated. For example, a father who, at the oedipal phase of development, may have hated his oedipal competitor might have been less enraged at his son at earlier stages of development. I am emphasizing the importance of phase-specific strain trauma and of serendipitously occurring, shockingly traumatic events in shaping individual destinies. A psychoanalytic perspective requires an exploration of each individual's past and his understanding of it rather than a decision as to the genesis of a disorder based on an assessment of the presenting symptomatology or the early transference manifestations. In that regard, the expression of what Kohut (1968) has described as a "mirror transference" may not reflect a recapitulation of arrested preoedipal development. It may, in selected cases, represent a transference regression from oedipal conflict.

Finally, it is important to emphasize the importance of postoedipal trauma in evoking dedifferentiation of psychic structure and regressive reorganization of a subject's character to preoedipal and oedipal modes of problem solving.

Brenner (1959) describes a woman in whom the serendipitous experience of shock traumas in adolescence and early adulthood revivified preoedipal and oedipal conflicts contributing significantly to this analysand's masochistic character organization:

> Both her father and brother died suddenly and bloodily. The former event was the more traumatic and the more significant for her masochistic character formation. It occurred when the patient was seventeen years old as the terminal event of a year's illness which was understood by the patient to be the consequence of many years of dissipation. Her father arose one morning, and had a massive hematemesis, and exsanguinated before the patient's eyes. Her brother killed himself some years later. The first of these two events contributed considerably to her unconscious guilt and to her fear that her murderous wishes could really kill, attitudes that were still further reinforced by her brother's death [p. 212–213].

Schucker (1979) describes similar regressive masochistic characterological reorganization in reasonably well-adjusted adult women in response to the shock trauma of their being helpless when overwhelmed by a violent rapist. There are also subjects whose development can be characterized as shaped by a traumatic process. The quality of their life experience has been far from optimal and has often approximated the traumatic. They have experienced strain trauma. These subjects, as well as those whose character organizations have been significantly influenced by shock traumas, may be thought of as having *traumatic character organizations*. They can be understood as, in part, either defending against anticipated traumas, recreating traumatic experiences, or attempting to undo past traumatic events. All diagnoses are at best only organizing rubrics that facilitate thinking about aspects of a patient. These subjects' personalities are, in part, organized "beyond the pleasure principle" and motivated by efforts to assimilate past traumatic experiences. While all human beings employ modes of defense of the type being considered, the issue is one of degree. Many, if not most, of the patients considered narcissistic personality disorders, masochistic characters, or acting-out characters have personalities that appear to be organized "beyond the pleasure principle" and to employ modes of problem solving and levels of ego organization associated with defenses of denial, projection, and externalization of superego introjects, as well as defensive narcissistic, masochistic, and sadistic identifications. I (1980a) have emphasized that narcissistic personality disorders, whose personalities are characterized by the prevalence of narcissistic defenses (i.e., by attempts to restore illusions of narcissistic perfection to the self-representation), can be found in a spectrum of integrations from psychotic to normal. The same can be said for this larger group of patients.

Berliner (1958) and Segal (1969) have elaborated Anna

Freud's concept of "identification with the aggressor." Their stress on the ego's employment of identificatory processes in its attempt to assimilate the traumatic introject presages an emphasis of this chapter. In regard to the genesis of masochism, Berliner (1958) describes "identification with the hater" (p. 49) and notes that "the original traumatic situation is reenacted by identification" (p. 48). Segal (1969) describes "identification with the doer" (p. 485) as a defense mechanism encountered in some patients with a tendency to act out. He relates this penchant to their efforts to master the trauma of intense, unexpected stimulation. Segal stresses real primalscene experiences, separations, and abandonments as frequently encountered traumatic determinants of such defensive identifications. In this regard, Stein (1973) is probably presenting such patients in his paper "Acting-out as a character trait." He describes them as a group of "neurotic characters" with a "tendency to act out" (p. 349)—a character trait he associates with magical thinking and serious, temporary lapses in reality testing and judgment.

A subject might develop such a character organization as the result of some combination of shock traumas or in response to the traumatic quality of his life—this latter quality influenced by the sum of a number of factors (the inborn biologic intensity of the instincts, the intactness of the ego organization, and the quality of the parents' availability and relatedness, particularly at specific phases of development). Particular phases of development, such as the rapprochement crisis, the oedipal phase, and preadolescence, are nodal points during which, in relatively short periods of time, profoundly important structuralizations occur. Such developmental milestones require specific qualities of parental relatedness for their optimal negotiation. Experiments of nature, such as deafness, remind us that a subject born with a compromised ego organization stresses a mother's and a family's capacity to respond in an optimal manner. I add this extreme example to avoid the kind of oversimplification which suggests that the traumas of development derive solely or primarily from the effects of disorders of maternal "empathy" in early phases of development.

These subjects, here described under the rubric *traumatic character organization,* have superegos perennially prone to threaten traumatic experience and their egos are significantly organized in response to their menacing superegos. Intense, prohibited feelings and associated wishes, as well as external events that represent the fulfillment of taboo wishes, threaten to evoke a traumatic superego response. These individuals have to cope not only with guilt and castration anxiety but also with fear of total destruction. These feelings derive from overdetermined memories of traumatic experiences from all levels of development, but emanating originally from preverbal states of mounting tension. Annie Reich (1960) lucidly describes these feeling states and refers to them as "feeling[s] of catastrophic annihilation" (p. 224). Such affects signal a panoply of defensive responses typically associated with the compulsion to repeat.

In analytic work with such subjects, the analyst's task is to facilitate the analysand's assimilation of traumas from all stages of development. For the analysand to assimilate his compulsion to repeat it is particularly important that he assimilate (1) his murderous rage, (2) his fear of his parents' murderous rage, (3) the elaboration of these factors in his developing superego, and (4) the defensive narcissistic, sadistic, and masochistic identifications commonly engendered by these terrifying perceptions and internalizations.

It is important to emphasize that these subjects' oedipal disappointments are often of traumatic proportions and remain active and unresolved. For example, the oedipal situation of one analysand, Mr. C (discussed below in Chapter 7) was traumatic. Any limits to his self-representation were experienced as traumatic – that is, as akin to annihilation because they represented, in part, the loss of the illusion of his special ("one and only") relationship to his mother. If he lost that organizing fantasy, he would have to remember a panoply of oedipal disappointments (reexperience an intensity of affectively laden memories that were transiently disorganizing). In addition, as long as he felt omnipotent, his mother's perfect narcissistic object, he would not end up like his father, shut out of the maternal bedroom, humiliated, and dead. Nor would he have to face his murderous rage or his paternal superego introject's wrathful envy and retaliating revenge.

It is important to emphasize that self-destructive repetitions are associated with a split in the self-representation; a split between the self-representation-as-agent and the self-representation-as-object. The suicidal subject says "I [self-representation-as-agent] am going to kill *my*self [self-representation-as-object]." Freud (1917a) alludes to this split when he suggests that "the analysis of melancholia now shows that the ego can kill itself only if, owing to the return of the object-cathexis, it can treat itself as an object" (p. 252). The narcissistically invested self-representation-as-agent, the "I," feels itself to be immortal and will kill the object. There are no words in the English language to express the murder of the "I." The subject cannot say "I'm going to kill I-self." The lack of appropriate language derives from a ubiquitous core narcissistic distortion in the self-representation.

# CHAPTER 5

# Narcissism

*As always... man has here again shown himself incapable of giving up a satisfaction he had once enjoyed. He is not willing to forgo the narcissistic perfection of his childhood.*

Sigmund Freud, *On Narcissism*

*Each of us... corrects some aspect of the world which is unbearable... by... a delusional remoulding of reality.*

Sigmund Freud, *Civilization and Its Discontents*

In the preceding chapter, the repetition compulsion is conceived to derive from an immature ego organization structured to assimilate traumatic experiences. Narcissism and masochism are elaborated as contents of psychic structure often employed by the ego in its defensive and assimilative endeavors. Chapters 5 and 6 present definitions of narcissism[1] and masochism to facilitate the organization of data that reflects these phenomena within the structural hypothesis.

Three-quarters of a century after psychoanalytic theory adopted the term *narcissism* from Greek mythology, analysts still differ as to its meaning. The term has been used within several theoretical frameworks for a variety of purposes. As a concept, it has been elaborated from libidinal and ego-psycho-

[1]Chapter 5 is a summary of definitions of narcissism and narcissistic personality disorder presented in my book *The Narcissistic Pursuit of Perfection*. A review of the literature is presented in that volume.

logical perspectives. It has been employed both descriptively and to connote developmental phenomena. It has been considered as a defensive function, and it has been characterized both as normal and ubiquitous and as one or another form of pathology. Much of this confusion can be seen to derive from the transitional nature of Freud's "war years" papers, in which he discusses structural development in terms inundated with metaphorical energic elaboration. The confusion between ego, self, and ego libido is still with us. It is characteristic of Freud's seminal papers that central terms and concepts have a variety of meanings. Freud (1914) defines *narcissism* as a quality of "perfection" (p. 94). In addition, he employs narcissism as a component of libido theory and uses it metaphorically to describe aspects of human development from the perspective of libido development. In his prestructural metapsychological papers, Freud organizes data within the libidinal concept of narcissism that will, subsequent to the introduction of the structural hypothesis, be discussed in terms of oral incorporative, defensive, identificatory responses of the ego. Thus Freud uses the term *narcissism* to describe a felt quality of perfection and as a prestructural concept to describe the development of psychic structure in response to ubiquitous narcissistic injuries. Confusion has resulted from these two very different developments of the meaning of the term and concept.

This book considers narcissism as different from the ego, the self, and the self-representation. These terms refer to aspects of psychic structure – each with a characteristic development. I propose that the definition of the term *narcissism* be limited to a felt quality of perfection. This conscious or unconscious, affectively laden fantasy may be invested in a panoply of self- and object representations in a spectrum of integrations.

The idea of perfection, or narcissistic perfection, should

encompass the libidinal concept primary narcissism, the object-representational concept self-object duality, and Andreas Salomé's (1921) "deep identification with the totality." The quality of perfection may be consciously pereceived or may be an unconsciously active, affectively valent fantasy. It is a ubiquitous aspect of human experience that facilitates distortion of one's sense of reality, particularly as this relates to one's sense of vulnerability and finiteness. It differs from person to person in its elaboration and integration by the ego.

Perfection is originally perceived during the preindividuated era. In that era, prior to a more defined and firmly established representational world, the quality of narcissistic perfection is felt to be part of the self that includes within it qualities of an object narcissistically perceived as perfect. All adult experiences of narcissistic perfection are built on the core of these original experiences; later experiences that capture a similar state of being are remembered and hierarchically organized in ever more abstract content in relationship to the original preindividuated experiences. For a given individual, the pursuit of perfection may be invested, for example, in phallic activities derived primarily from oedipal issues and conflicts. However, whatever the narcissistic investment, it is associatively linked to preindividuated fixation points of perfection that remain unconscious and in a state of primary repression. These shape and influence all subsequent investments. A variety of affective signals may provoke ego elaboration, the result being a spectrum of possible integrations within a variety of psychic structures.

The content of narcissistic perfection, as experienced by an adult, usually has affective, physical, and cognitive components. The cognitive component is the conception of perfection, expressed in ideas of omniscience or omnipotence. A subject or object may be thought of as most knowing, most powerful, most beautiful, most successful, etc. What is common to all is a superlative designation, such as "most" and the absolute quality of this designation. Perfection is also associated with the number "one," and often with the wish to be "one and only."

A variety of affects are linked to these conceptions. When narcissistic perfection is felt to be part of the self-representation, the subject's positive self-esteem is experienced along a spectrum from well-being to elation. These feelings are often associated with a physical sense that the subject's body is functioning well. When narcissistic perfection is felt to be an attribute of the object, the subject may feel some degree of reverence or awe. By performing successfully for the narcissistically invested object, a subject feels a sense of positive self-esteem. A similar affective response is often associated with a subject's living up to the standards of his ego ideal or superego.

A discussion of the content of narcissistic perfection should be complemented by a description of its form and integration in self- and object representations, in ego functions and activities, and in such psychic structures as the ego ideal. The motives and affective signals that provoke the pursuit of perfection include a spectrum of real and imagined dangers, as well as painful and disappointing perceptions. Signal anxieties, and the often associated feelings of rage, disappointment, or sexual excitement, may motivate a subject to pursue one or another form of narcissistic perfection.

The term *narcissistic* can refer to an aspect of a number of experiences, processes, and situations. Narcissistic gratification refers to a subject's experience of perfection; narcissistic injury, to a subject's experience of the loss of perfection. The experience of any limit to the self-representation can be linked associatively to the original perception of limits and of lost narcissistic perfection. The rage associated with such an injury has been referred to as narcissistic rage (Kohut, 1972). Rage is also experienced when an object who has been narcissistically invested disappoints a subject who feels entitled to the presence of an idealized object. The ego process of attributing narcissistic perfection to something is referred to as narcissistic investment. The choice of the word *investment* is intended to connote a process whereby a quality is added to something. When the investment is in the self-representation, it is accomplished by a process of narcissistic identification. When an object is perceived as narcissistically perfect, it is referred to as a narcissistic object (animate or inanimate). A regressive shift in the integration of a subject's narcissistic investments is designated a narcissistic regression.

The defensive investment of perfection in the analysand's self-representation in response to an analytic intervention or to the threat of progress in the analytic situation is referred to as narcissistic resistance. The mirror and the idealizing transferences described by Kohut (1968, p. 88), which represent an attempt to recapitulate an aspect of structural development in the analytic situation, are referred to as narcissistic transferences. Kohut's valuable clinical descriptions refer, however, to more than narcissistic issues; his (1977) recent designation of these phenomena as "self-object transferences" (p. xiv) reflects his awareness of this fact. From the perspective of the structural hypothesis, the mirror transference can be viewed as an attempt by the analysand to recapture a sense of the original narcissistic perfection for the self-representation, but this transference reflects repetitions that derive from both preoedipal and oedipal conflicts. Preoedipal conflicts, often resulting in disturbed integration of primary identifications, are influenced by the nature of the subject's maturing character organization and by the relatedness of the primary object. It is important to note that these transference phenomena can be motivated in regressive defensive flight from intense oedipal conflicts. They may reflect wishes for a particular kind of paternal "mirroring," or responsiveness, that derives from both preoedipal and oedipal conflicts with the paternal object.

Similarly, the idealizing transference reflects the analysand's efforts to invest the object representation of the analyst with illusions of narcissistic perfection. Again, in contradiction to Kohut, these transference phenomena often are manifestations of much more than preoedipal developmental interferences. Frequently, they are an aspect of intense oedipal transference trends that reflect disorders of superego structuralization.

A more limited definition of narcissism need not result in loss; it may, rather, facilitate a number of distinctions that contribute to more precise communication. For example, the term *narcissism* is different from the terms *self* and *self-representation*. It is a perceived quality that may be experienced as part of the self-representation. In this sense, self-involvement is not equivalent to narcissistic involvement. The former may refer to any self-oriented activity in which the subject engages. The latter term refers to activity limited to the pursuit of illusions of narcissistic perfection in one or another form.

The definition being elaborated in this chapter is a unitary one. It views all narcissistic perfection as the same. Narcissistic perfection is a defensive distortion of reality – an affectively laden fantasy based on the original perfection of the self-object bliss of the symbiotic phase. Its loss is a ubiquitous developmental insult from which few, if any, human beings ever recover. Freud's (1923a) formulations of ego development are based on the above perception: "It may be that this identification is the sole condition under which the id can give up its objects" (p. 29). Mahler (1972) similarly emphasizes this point: "One could regard the entire life cycle as . . . an eternal longing for the actual or fantasied 'ideal state of self,' with the latter standing for a symbiotic fusion with the 'all good' symbiotic mother, who was at one time part of the self in a blissful state of well-being" (p. 338).

Freud's statement can be elaborated, integrating the contributions of Kohut and Mahler, to read: narcissistically invested identification is the sole condition under which the id can give up its objects and is a fundamental concomitant of primary separation-individuation. The pursuit of narcissistic perfection in one form or another is a defensive distortion that is a ubiquitous characteristic of the ego. It is a goal of analysis to identify the nature of the analysand's narcissistic investments and to work through those aspects of the investments that contribute to suffering and maladaptation. It is questionable whether the total relinquishment of narcissistic perfection is possible or desirable.

The proposed definition is intended to facilitate a dynamic perspective. It should help an analyst accept his own and his analysand's narcissism as inevitable, more similar than different, and of potentially pleasurable and social value. This view of narcissism should facilitate a number of questions. What percepts and painful affects stimulate an analysand's pursuit of perfection? What painful memories does an analysand's continued pursuit of perfection protect him from remembering or reexperiencing? What fears and frightening perceptions (his own death, the death of a loved one, his own or the object's murderous rage, castration, loss of love, etc.) does the pursuit of perfection shield the analysand from?

Narcissism is neither healthy nor pathologic. Relatively healthy or pathologic egos integrate narcissism in a healthy or pathologic manner. Such a perspective is of heuristic value for a number of reasons. First, it is based on an appreciation of the ubiquitous defensive nature of all narcissistic investment. Second, it is in greater harmony with the developing ego-psychological perspective of the structural theory proposed by Freud and elaborated by numerous others. Third, it mitigates against a common countertransference potential to respond pejoratively to a subject whose narcissism an analyst may consider pathological.

In regard to the second point, I have suggested that Freud is moving in this direction and that it is implicit in his formulations, as it is explicit in the writings of Wilhelm Reich (1933), that all character is in part defensive and that illusions of narcissistic perfection are integrated within those structured defenses of the ego referred to as "character."

It is the ego that develops and not narcissism. An ego developing in a healthy manner facilitates a subject's experience of some significant degree of object love, of productive and humanistic work, and of satisfying self-involvement and play. Such an ego integrates its pursuit of narcissistic perfection in a manner that facilitates these pursuits. In addition, it is associated with an investment of narcissistic perfection in an ego ideal that finds some significant degree of harmony with the subject's self-representation and that contributes to a tone of positive self-esteem. Pathologic ego development is often associated with a more rigid, compulsive pursuit of narcissistic perfection – either for one's self-representation or in objects – in a form that is unattainable, isolating, and maladaptive and that, by virtue of these characteristics, is associated with fluctuations of mood. It is the ego, and not narcissism, that develops in a manner that permits a relatively more or less harmonious relationship with reality. The relatively healthy ego integrates its pursuits of narcissistic perfection in a manner that is in harmony with its endowments and the opportunities for identification and for gratification available in reality. The distortions of reality implicit in all narcissistic pursuits are integrated by such an ego in a manner that does not result in disharmony and maladaption. These integrations often remain unchallenged or are only challenged when the subject faces death or some profound threat to his character integration.

The distinction between pathologic and normal ego development is more consistent with the data and less vulnerable to pejorative elaboration. There has been a tendency to judge different forms of narcissistic pursuit as more or less healthy. For example, the pursuit of narcissistic perfection for one's body has been considered less healthy than the pursuit of perfection for one's mind. Similarly, the pursuit of perfection in a humanitarian profession has been considered healthier than the pursuit of perfection in the performing arts. Such distinctions are clearly oversimplifications. What is required in assessing health and illness is a much more complex assessment of psychic structure—its adaptive or maladaptive relation to reality—as well as the subject's experience of his reality.

The present controversy concerning patients with narcissistic disturbances is reflected in the many descriptive and diagnostic labels used to refer to them: narcissistic character, phallic-narcissistic character, narcissistic character disorder, narcissitic personality, and narcissistic personality disorder. In addition the current controversy concerning diagnosis is influenced by the fact that, while some analysts favor strictly defined diagnostic categories, others are less concerned with the question of classification. Different authors stress different aspects of the integration of narcissism, and various authors employ the same terms for different purposes without explicitly stating the distinctions. Thus, using different frames of reference, different authors refer to seemingly different groups of patients as, in some way, "narcissistic."

At the present time, analysts tend to think of narcissistic patients in terms of Kernberg's or Kohut's explications of these disorders. Many find aspects of their contributions valuable and creative, as well as confusing, and strive to integrate and preserve the contributions of both. Much of the unclarity derives from Kernberg's and Kohut's failure to differentiate narcissism from ego, superego, and ego-ideal development. The limited definition of narcissism as a felt quality of perfection stresses the ubiquity of narcissistic investments and allows for an appreciation of the panoply of contents and integrations of narcissism in the "character" of the ego. It permits an ego-psychological definition of narcissistic personality disorder, as well as a classificatory schema of all narcissistic investments. A narcissistic personality disorder is defined by the predominant mode of investment of narcissism in the self-representation. This diagnostic designation, based on an appreciation of the predominant mode of investment, should be complemented by a consideration of its state of integration along a spectrum from psychotic to normal.

The definitions and classificatory schema proposed in this chapter derive from a hypothetical, representational, and structural perspective that is an ego-psychological synthesis of Freud's ideas on narcissism and on the genesis of "character" as presented in his seminal works *On Narcissism: An Introduction* and *The Ego and the Id.*

There is heuristic value in maintaining the diagnostic designation narcissistic personality disorder, but it should be integrated with Freud's (1914) observation of man's ubiquitous defensive attempt to preserve illusions of his primary narcissism. Wilhelm Reich (1933) explicitly elaborates this proposition in his conception of character as "essentially a narcissistic protection mechanism." His diagnostic category of the phallic-narcissistic character (pp. 201–207) represents an exploration of a specific mode of investment of narcissism in various states of integration – a mode typically encountered in certain male patients.

The perspective presented here, which stresses that all people are narcissistic, is an extension of that proposed by Freud, Reich, and Kohut. What is required is a definition of the term *narcissistic personality disorder* and a complementary psychoanalytic classification of narcissism in the "character" (Freud, 1923a) of the ego. Any classificatory schema must be limited and incomplete for it can only be a partial reflection of what are always more complex human phenomena. Nevertheless, an effort at clarifying the classifying rubrics employed to describe the panoply of expressions of narcissism in the human situation is of potential heuristic and clinical value. The present classification is based on an extension and elaboration of Kohut's construct of two different modes of narcissistic investment. This classification emphasizes the ubiquitous nature of narcissistic investment and attempts to consider both its predominant mode of investment and its state of integration.

A narcissistic personality disorder is defined by the predominant mode of investment of narcissism in the self-representation. Wilhelm Reich's phallic-narcissistic characters, as well as Kernberg's narcissistic personalities, would be considered narcissistic personality disorders in this classification. In contrast to Kohut's, this diagnostic designation is not based on transference phenomena. A secondary diagnostic statement that reflects a consideration of the state of structural integration of narcissism is necessary. Again in contrast to Kohut, it is proposed that the narcissistic personality disorder can be seen in psychotic, borderline, neurotic, and "normal" states of integration. Following the perspective of Arlow and Brenner (1964), these categories are seen as representing a spectrum within which fluidity is possible.

A second possible mode of investment is in object representations. When the predominant mode of investment is in object representations and when the subject's ego has developed the degree of differentiation associated with well-integrated ego-ideal and superego structuralizations, the result is the traditional neurotic or normal character integration of narcissism. There are patients, however, whose psychic structures do not develop to that degree and whose predominant mode of investment is still in object representations. As with the narcissistic personality disorder, this investment may be found along a spectrum of integrations from psychotic to normal. A predominant mode of investment in object representations is often associated with a suppliant, passive, or seductive attitude on the part of the subject toward its narcissistically invested object. This suppliant attitude may be elaborated and complemented by masochistic content (in which the subject may feel the perfect sufferer) in order to gain the attention and approval of the idealized object. It is worth considering the term *suppliant personality disorder* to describe patients whose predominant mode of narcissistic investment is in object representations.

Narcissistic investment in object representations is implicit in the traditional diagnosis of neurosis in that neurotic and normal people delegate their lost narcissistic perfection to their ego ideals. Defensive pursuits of illusions of perfection are more easily denied when they are only implicit or when they are subsumed under such terms as "normal narcissism." The term *suppliant personality disorder* emphasizes the tenacious and ubiquitous nature of man's hunger for illusions of perfection. It emphasizes that all human beings pursue these illusions in one or another mode. What is different is the state of integration of these pursuits along a spectrum from psychotic to normal.

What has been called normal narcissism, in contrast to normal self-esteem or self-regard, is a mechanism for self-aggrandizement and subtle self-delusion that man finds necessary to assuage the insult of his true being. This perspective emphasizes the irrational, interminable nature of man's pursuit of perfection.

The felt quality of perfection is a ubiquitous illusion created by the ego of the toddler in response to the inevitable limits of development experienced as traumatic. The narcissistic illusion is created from memories of pleasurable experiences. Appreciation of the parent as pain rendering, enraged, or sadistic is defended against by denial, projection, externalization, and splitting of the self- and object-representations. Masochism and the primary masochistic experience can be understood as a similar and complementary developmental experience. The ego in creating the ubiquitous masochistic illusion, also integrates the perception of the unavailable, absent, pain rendering, enraged, or sadistic parent. In doing so the ego preserves the illusion of its original narcissistic perfection. In that sense masochism can be understood as a more complex and convoluted narcissistic distortion of reality. Human beings are able to employ masochistic defenses and pursue masochistic gratifications because they believe that it is all an illusion orchestrated by the narcissistically invested self-representation-as-agent.

# CHAPTER 6

# Masochism

> *There remains an uneasy suspicion that this is not a
> final solution to the problem [of masochism]....But
> impressions of this kind, as I know from my own ex-
> perience are only too willingly put on one side.*
> Sigmund Freud, *A Child Is Being Beaten*

Masochism remains the most enigmatic phenomenon in
the human condition. Along with the related problems of
sadism of the superego and negative therapeutic reaction, it
contributes to many interminable and less than optimal analytic results. The purpose of this chapter is to clarify the
theory of masochism and provide a more felicitous understanding of masochistic phenomena within an evolving structural hypothesis. Although most authors note its overdetermined nature, they stress one or another aspect of masochistic
phenomena in their explications. Masochism is defined in various ways. It is understood to derive from energic, dynamic-
genetic, or adaptive-defensive roots. Masochistic phenomena
is said to exhibit a spectrum of integrations within the human
condition.

This chapter conceives of masochism as a content[1] of
structure in the service of defense and as an aspect of character organization. Masochism derives from the integration of
the child's narcissistic strivings with his experience of painful

[1] In *The Narcissistic Pursuit of Perfection,* I suggest the advantages of
conceiving of narcissism in a similar manner.

discomfort and perceptions of parents as angry, sadistic, humiliating, pain-rendering, or unavailable (absent, dead, etc.).

Masochism troubles and intrigues Freud because some of its manifestations seem to contradict the pleasure principle. Freud ultimately understands masochistic phenomena to be "beyond the pleasure principle," to derive from biology – from thanatos, the death instinct. Freud's brilliance, in part, derives from his humility. He is courageous enough to propose the creative eros-thanatos theory and also sufficiently humble and realistic to acknowledge its speculative and hypothetical nature. In *The Ego and the Id* he states that "there is . . . no doubt about the pleasure principle, . . . but the distinction between two classes of instincts does not seem sufficiently assured and it is possible that facts of clinical analysis may be found which will do away with its pretension" (p. 42).

Throughout his writing Freud notes his dissatisfaction with his formulations concerning masochism. In *Three Essays:* "All that need be said is that no satisfactory explanation of this perversion has been put forward *and that it seems possible that a number of mental impulses are combined in it to produce a single resultant*" (p. 159, emphasis added). In his last clinical study of the subject (1919): "There remains an uneasy suspicion that this is not a final solution to the problem. . . . To a great extent these [beating] phantasies subsist apart from the rest of the content of a neurosis, and find no proper place in its structure. But impressions of this kind, as I know from my own experience, are only too willingly put on one side" (p. 183).

Masochism is defined as the experience of pleasure in pain, and fundamental questions derive from attempts to understand the nature of this pleasure. Freud (1905) early notes that various definitions for these enigmatic phenomena derive from differing perspectives. In *Three Essays* he presents a variety of definitions: "Schrenck-Notzing . . . preferred the narrower term 'algolagnia.' This emphasizes the pleasure in pain, the cruelty" (p. 157). And, strikingly contemporary in its object-relations implications: "The desire to inflict pain upon a sexual object – and its reverse – received from Krafft-Ebing the names 'sadism' and 'masochism' for its active and passive forms respectively. [These] bring into prominence the pleasure in any form of humiliation or subjection" (p. 157).

Freud (1924) describes three types of masochism, "an *erotogenic,* a *feminine,* and a *moral* masochism." Erotogenic masochism is synonymous with primary masochism and the death instinct. It "lies at the bottom of the other two forms. Its basis must be sought along biologic and constitutional lines and it remains incomprehensible unless one decides to make certain assumptions about matters that are extremely obscure" (p. 161). He proposes that very early in life there occurs "a libidinal sympathetic excitation when there is tension due to pain and unpleasure" (p. 163). This becomes "an infantile physiologic mechanism [that] provide[s] the physiological foundation on which the psychical structure of erotogenic masochism [will] afterwards be erected" (p. 163).

In *A Child Is Being Beaten,* Freud (1919) describes a three-layered meaning to beating fantasies: (1) "My father is beating the child *whom I hate"* (p. 185). (2) *"I am being beaten by my father"* (p. 185). (3) "A stranger, a representative of the father, such as a teacher" (p. 185), is beating a child or a number of children while the analysand reports "I am probably looking on" (p. 186). Freud notes that the "second phase is the most important, . . . but . . . it has never had a real existence. It is never remembered, it has never succeeded in becoming conscious. It is a construction of analysis" (p. 185).

Freud (1924) also describes other aspects of masochistic longing. He notes that "the masochist wants to be treated like a small and helpless child, but particularly, like a naughty child" (p. 162). These wishes "place the subject in a characteristically female situation; they signify, that is, being castrated, or copulated with, or giving birth to a baby" (p. 162).

Freud discusses nuances of the dynamics and genetics of masochistic phenomena. While his clear emphasis is on oedipal factors in the genesis of female and moral masochism, he (1905) does note preoedipal influences: "According to some authorities this aggressive element of the sexual instinct is in reality a relic of cannibalistic desires – that is, *it is a contribution derived from the apparatus for obtaining mastery,* which is concerned with the satisfaction of the other and, ontogenetically, *the older of the great instinctual needs"* (p. 189, emphasis added). This presages a line of thought that Freud will delineate, but again will not emphasize, in his explication of phenomena organized "beyond the pleasure principle." In a footnote to this 1905 passage, added to the text in 1915, Freud indicates that his larger work "on the pregenital phases of sexual development confirm this view" (p. 159n). In 1919, he suggests that constitutional factors predispose to a "pregenital, sadistic-anal organization of . . . sexual life" (p. 189) that is the fixation point for regressive beating fantasies and oedipally derived masochism.

"*It is not only the punishment for the forbidden genital relation, but also the regressive substitute for that relation* [that is] the essence of masochism" (p. 189). The emphasis is clearly oedipal: "The Oedipus complex is the actual nucleus of neuroses, and the infantile sexuality which culminates in this complex is the true determinant of neuroses. . . . The beating-phantasies . . . would only be precipitates of the Oedipus complex, scars . . . left behind after the process has ended" (p. 193).

Freud (1919) states that these oedipally derived beating fantasies "provide a means for masturbatory satisfaction" (p. 186), and Brenner (1959) interprets him to be saying that they are "a *condition* for sexual pleasure rather than . . . that they give rise to pleasure directly" (p. 198). In this treatment of masochism, Freud also adds that it is to "a certain extent narcissistic" (p. 194), alluding, I think, to its employment in defense against assimilating the narcissistic humiliation of oedipal defeat.

Freud's more definitive understanding of masochism derives from and rests upon more experience-distant energic hypotheses. Prior to 1920 (Freud, 1905, 1915, 1919), masochism has been understood to be derived from sadism. In *Instincts and their Vicissitudes,* Freud proposes that masochism is an example of "reversal of an instinct into its opposite. . . . Masochism is actually sadism turned round upon the subject's own ego [self]" (p. 127). In 1920 Freud states that "the account that was formerly given of masochism requires emendation as being too sweeping in one respect: there *might* be such a thing as primary masochism" (p. 55). He speculates that primary masochism (the death instinct) is acted upon by narcissistic libido (the life instinct) and that a fusion of libido and destrudo result in sadism. Sadism turned upon the self is a secondary masochistic phenomenon: "Sadism is in fact a death instinct which, under the influence of narcissistic libido, has been forced away from the ego and has consequently only emerged in relation to the object. . . . [Secondary] masochism, the turning round of the instinct upon the subject's own ego, would . . . be . . . a regression" (pp. 54–55).

Finally, it is important to emphasize that the death instinct,[2] primary masochism (1920), and erotogenic masochism

[2] Although the hypothesis of the death instinct finds few contemporary advocates, it is of interest to note that some of our most creative colleagues (Alexander, 1929; Bergler, 1961; and M. Klein, 1933) accept the concept and integrate it into their contributions: "Biological considerations, however, demand the assumption of a death-instinct in an unequivocal way. From the beginning of life the disintegrative nidus of the elements of the highly complex biological molecule is active within it. It constitutes the core of the self-destructive tendencies upon which the later ones of the ego and the super-ego are deposited. It is then merely a question of convention from what point onward one talks of a death-instinct. . . .

"The surface tension which arrests the growth of the drop of liquid and disrupts it, the decomposition of the biological molecule into its elements

(1924) are synonyms. They emphasize Freud's belief that masochism is fundamentally a biologically derived phenomenon. As he states in 1924: "Erotogenic masochism accompanies the libido through all its developmental phases and derives from them its changing psychical coatings" (pp. 164–165).

All contributors to our understanding of masochism have emphasized its complexity and overdetermined nature. Most, however, stress one or another factor in their discussions of these phenomena. All acknowledge the importance of constitutional factors in the genesis of these phenomena, and most, with the exception of Bergler, would agree with Arlow's opinion concerning the concepts eros and thanatos: "Such biological speculations are undesirable in the context of clinical discussions, since they involve extrapolations which are incapable of confirmation or contradiction in this setting" (Stein, 1956, p. 526).

I have organized select post-Freudian contributions into three groups: (1) those that stress the influence of the object world, (2) those that emphasize the quality of the object as traumatic, such traumas being experienced as narcissistic injury, and (3) those that emphasize, affirm, and elaborate the factors that Freud has stressed in his clinical comments on the subject. The first two groups approach masochism from the perspective of an ego functioning "beyond the pleasure principle."

In a series of articles, Berliner (1940, 1942, 1947, 1958) emphasizes the fundamental importance of the aggression and sadism of the preoedipal parental object in the genesis of

---

during the katabolic phase of metabolism, the self-destruction of the psychic apparatus, the breaking up of states and cultures: all these are expressions of the same regressive dynamic principle, which counteracts growth and life just as the momentum of inertia opposes the formation of higher dynamic units, and which we should all so much like to forget or deny in its biological manifestation as the death instinct" (Alexander, 1929, p. 269).

masochism: "The ill-treating parent does not belong to the dim prehistoric past.... This parent... is still very much alive" (p. 43). Masochism is "a disturbance of object relations, a pathologic way of loving a person who gives hate and ill-treatment" (p. 40). It is the "solution of an infantile conflict ... on the level of oral and skin eroticism.... It is a defensive structure against the need for love and the experience of non-love" (p. 10). He stresses the role of defensive "identification with the hater" (p. 49) as essential to the masochist's adaptation, and he describes the "introjection of another person's sadism [as its] essential pattern" (p. 51). "The original traumatic situation is reenacted by *identification* in the masochist with the frustrating love object.... The analysis of this part of the masochistic character is the most important part of our work" (p. 48).

Socarides (1958) meaningfully elaborates the child's defensive response to the perception of parental hate and sadism and to what are ultimately unconsciously perceived as infanticidal wishes. There is *"denial* of the perception of hatefulness on the part of the sought-for-love object.... The true perception of hate is too great a danger to the patient, threatening him with abandonment and release of rage.... Blaming the self instead of blaming the parent is the safest solution" (p. 592).

Valenstein (1973) also emphasizes the quality of the pre-oedipal object as the essential factor in the negative therapeutic reaction potential of a number of patients who are deeply attached "to pain" (p. 366): "The negative therapeutic reaction... the attachment to pain – I might even say, in terms of masochism as well as the instinctual drives, the fixation to pain – generally suggests a major problem in object tie from the first year of life and thereafter" (p. 373). This pain helps maintain the integrity of the ego. "Such affects are emphatically held to because they represent the early self and self-object" (p. 376). The implication is that the masochist has had an early experience of a pain-rendering object and that in some way, for these individuals, pain is experienced as the object and is required to maintain the integration of their representational worlds. "Attachment to pain signifies an original attachment to painfully experienced objects and inconstant objects at that" (p. 389).

Sacks and Miller's (1975) discussion of some "biological influences on masochistic behavior" (p. 250) is helpful in understanding Valenstein's fascinating clinical material. They report Hess's observation that a painful stimulus to an infant chick "increases attraction rather than decreasing it" (p. 250) and Rosenblum and Harlow's (1963) classic study of infant monkeys given free access to a cloth surrogate mother. "Two of the monkeys were exposed to a forty-five second blast of air while on the surrogate. The result showed that the 'punished' monkeys spent significantly longer time with the surrogate than did the subjects that were not punished" (p. 250). They note that "this experiment supports the notion that a cruel mother may elicit stronger attachment from her young than a gentle one" (p. 250). Freud has emphasized that the immature psychic apparatus is organized beyond the pleasure principle. From the metaphorical perspective of Freud's stimulus barrier, Harlow's monkeys' stimulus barriers were clearly overloaded. It may be a biological response of an immature infant to cling to and become attached to a pain-rendering parent in the preprogrammed "belief" that such a response is adaptive and favors survival. It is also possible that defensive operations of an immature ego – such as splitting of fragile, tenuously structuralized self- and object-representations, denial, projection of rage, and externalization of introjects – are available early in life and facilitate and complement the infant's and toddler's adaptive strivings.

Menaker (1953) deepens our understanding of the nature and effects of a disturbance in the primary object's relatedness to the developing child's masochism. Adumbrating

Kohut's (1977) emphasis, Menaker conceives of a deprivation of maternal affirmation of the growing ego functions.

> Failing this the demands of the ego are associated with pain ... and are ultimately hated. When such elemental functions as walking, speaking, feeding oneself, etc., are not permitted to develop normally because of neurotic attitudes of the mother [lack of optimal responsiveness and affirmation], self-hate and the feeling of powerlessness... appear very early, [and]... masochistic self-devaluation... functions as a defense against experiencing this deprivation with its concomitant anxiety and aggression, and that it is a means of perpetuating whatever bond there is to the mother [pp. 208–209].

In a complex and comprehensive paper Loewenstein (1957) emphasizes the importance of parental aggression and a disturbance in preoedipal object relations in the genesis of masochism. He is, however, faithful to Freud in his statement that the "appearance of the masochistic *perversion* [is] never before the oedipal period" (p. 208, emphasis added): "The masochistic scene is thus a means of gratifying the forbidden, repressed incestuous fantasies, but with the castration threat undone" (p. 202). He stresses the role of trauma (p. 205) in his discussion of the development of beating fantasies in a particular analysand. Most important, he emphasizes the role of the toddler's ego in assimilating the perception of parental aggression in the development of "protomasochism" during the preoedipal epoch. He explains as the "seduction of the aggressor" the toddler's "seeking for situations that entail danger, fear and unpleasure, and their attenuation through a loving, erotic complicity of the threatening person.... These games ... resemble the patterns... in masochistic perversions" (p. 215). He avoids the theoretical contradiction in this statement by suggesting that "it is... appropriate to term it *proto or premasochism* as long as any involvement of the genital apparatus is absent" (p. 216). Finally he stresses that a complexity of factors, derived from preoedipal and oedipal development events and conflicts in the genesis of masochistic phenomena, contribute to a panoply of expressions of masochism in a spectrum of ego integrations:

> There are nuances of masochism where one of the factors, i.e., the reinforced erotogenic masochism, has greater importance, and others in which the role of the 'legacy' of the Oedipus complex" predominates. The former would obtain when enjoyment of physical pain is the essential point, the latter when enjoyment of threats and humiliation is the condition for gratification. In cases where the 'legacy of the Oedipus complex' is of little importance, masochism or other perversions might also be due to a severe disorder of the ego in the area of object relations [pp. 227–228].

Bernstein (1957) has elaborated yet another aspect of the role played by disturbance in object relations in the genesis of masochism: the "parental narcissistic and sadistic attitudes toward" (p. 374) the infant and young child. He suggests that in response to the perception of the hostile quality of the parents' narcissistic investment, the child resorts to masochistic fantasies and "narcissistic defiance" (p. 373) to cope with their painful disappointments. "The consequence for many children so conditioned is that failure and defeat become triumphant in childhood" (p. 373). "These fantasies in masochistic behavior may be considered to be, in part, a defense against the traumatic feelings of loss, helplessness, annihilation or castration" (p. 375).

Bergler, in a prolific production of papers and books, conceives of masochism as the unifactorial fundament of all neurotic suffering. He provocatively proclaims that he has the answer. Colleagues who cannot understand his proposals are suffering from countertransference problems. Although this polemical perspective has influenced his writing style and contributed to his colleagues' lack of interest in his work, there is significant value in some of his theoretical propositions. His last book, *Curable and Incurable Neurotics,* is rich in clinical descriptions that are particularly helpful. He accepts the death instinct as biologic masochism and distinguishes a "psychic" masochism whose genesis he places between four to eighteen months of life which corresponds to Mahler's (et al., 1975) psychological "hatching" of the human infant from "symbiosis."

Bergler conceives of masochism as a ubiquitous developmental defense of an ego struggling to maintain the illusion of "its original narcissistic perfection." *"It is my contention that the first and foremost conflict of the newborn, infant, baby, consists in the fact that he must come to terms with his inborn megalomania. That conflict invariably and without exception results in a masochistic solution, the 'pleasure-in-displeasure pattern.' This constitutes the 'basic neurosis'"* (1961, p. 63). The "protracted helplessness of childhood" (p. 52) inevitably results in some psychic tension, while parents, in the process of setting limits, impose further injury to the child's sense of perfection. To master this the toddler constructs his superego: "In his frantic effort to hold on to vestiges of his most cherished infantile fantasy – omnipotence, megalomania, autarchy – the child of two or two-and-a-half . . . substitutes an *inner* prohibition for the barrage of *external* prohibitions" (p. 32). Once having created the superego, the masochist tortures himself to assuage or disarm the feared sadism of the torturing superego. Thus masochism becomes the "crime of crimes," a defiant, narcissistically invested pleasure in "the neutralization of the superego's power" (p. 80).

From an object-relations perspective that is strikingly similar to Bergler's, Eidelberg (1959) focuses on the "unpleasure," the "narcissistic mortification," the ubiquitous experiences of limits that are experienced as humiliations. These mortifications he defines as "a sudden loss of control over internal or external reality caused by the force of internal or external 'enemies'" (pp. 274–275).

From a Berglerian perspective, Eidelberg proposes that

defeat, failure, and punishment have "a humiliating meaning" (p. 276). He points out that the masochist does not seek "unpleasure ... in order to achieve finally pleasure but ... to deny the presence of an unconscious internal narcissistic mortification" (p. 287). The humiliator is the superego, and the masochist, to paraphrase Anna Freud (1936) and Sandler (1960), identifies with the humiliator and imposes on himself the humiliation he expects, thereby eliminating the anticipated narcissistic mortification of being humiliated by the superego. Eidelberg concludes that it is as if the masochist were saying "I can always succeed in provoking a humiliating defeat and retain in that way my infantile omnipotence" (p. 283).

Recently, Arlow (1980), in a fascinating paper, has described the experience of the limits associated with primal-scene perceptions as a "deep narcissistic mortification" (p. 529). He notes that "closely connected with the feelings stemming from narcissistic mortification is the impulse of the hapless observer of the primal scene to wreak vengeance on one or both of the betraying parents" (p. 523). I would add that in the process of such sadistic vengeful pursuits the mortified subject often imposes masochistic or self-destructive gratification upon himself.

In a lucid article, Parkin (1980) extends Bergler's and Eidelberg's focus on the narcissistic aspects of masochistic experience:

> The basic state ... in masochism is ... enthrallment [p. 307].
> ... I find Eidelberg's emphasis upon the masochist's early narcissistic mortification absolutely central, but I would instead stress the masochist's *attempt to recover the lost omnipotence in fantasy through striving for the maternal self-ideal of the grandeur of power and the fascination of fury* [p. 309]. ... The basic structure of the masochistic character consists of a self-ideal made up of grossly over-estimated and ambivalently regarded maternal introjects, particularly of a phallic nature, and an ego made up of sexually degraded self-images [p.

311].... When what is conscious and emphasized are the erotic qualities of the over-estimated and ambivalently regarded maternal ideal introjects or their paternal phallic successors, ... the state is ... sexual enthrallment.... When what is conscious and emphasized are the aggressive qualities, ... the state is ... masochistic enthrallment [pp. 311–312].... The power and grandeur which has been ceded out of the original state of primary narcissism to the ideal in the state of enthrallment may be recovered by the debased ego through identification with it [p. 312].

Kohut (1968) has discussed similar issues in his elaboration of the "idealizing transference," and I (1980a) have commented upon such relationships within the rubric of "suppliant personality disorders."

Kohut, like Bergler, obfuscates what is of value in his contribution by his insistence on a unifactorial explanation of the vast majority of clinical data. The validity of his propositions seems for Kohut to derive, in part, from a critical view of drive theory:

The essence of sadism and masochism ... is not the expression of a primary destructive or self-destructive tendency, of a primary biologic drive that can only secondarily be kept in check through fusion, neutralization, and other means; it is a two-step process: After the breakup of the primary psychological unit (assertively demanded empathy-merger with the self-object), the drive appears as a disintegration product; the drive is then enlisted in the attempt to bring about the lost merger (and thus the repair of the self) by pathologic means, i.e., as enacted in the fantasies and actions of the perverts [p. 128].

Brenner (1959) from a traditional Freudian perspective stresses the overdetermined nature of masochistic phenomena. His emphasis is clearly oedipal: "Masochistic character traits and fantasies are a legacy of infantile sexual conflicts, principally of oedipal conflicts in most cases" (p. 225). His definition of masochism is within the pleasure principle. Masochism is "the seeking of unpleasure for the sake of *sexual* pleasure" (p. 197). The "pain is a *condition* for sexual pleasure" (p. 198). Bak (1946) presents a case of psychotically integrated masochism. In fealty to Freud, Bak emphasizes oedipal dynamics in the genesis of his patient's masochism; however, he also emphasizes the traumatic effects of both parents' personalities in influencing his patient's psychotic integration. "In paranoia the sadism is turned largely into its opposite, into masochism" (p. 257). "The patient's delusional elaborations, as being mistreated, injured and persecuted, gratify the original masochistic desires of castration, beating and abuse by the father. The delusion is a return of the repressed, and *paranoia is delusional masochism"* (p. 297). Although Bak derives his patient's masochism from a "constitutional predisposition" (p. 293) organized at the level of the "negative Oedipus" (p. 293), he notes the profound influence of the parents' personalities in shaping his patient's personality organization: "His bisexuality was supplemented by his mother's harsh treatment. . . . These factors resulted in an identification with . . . the aggressive phallic mother [and] he turned to the father to be loved and appreciated by him" (p. 293). His father's rejection precipitates his paranoid regression as an effort at establishing an object relationship. This explanation is in the spirit of Freud's (1911c) explication of the restitutive function of Schreber's delusions.

Before proceeding with my exploration of these issues, it is worth noting that Freud's discussions of masochism leave much to be desired because more than any aspect of his brilliant contribution these rely considerably on experience-distant energic hypotheses. Early in his work, in *The Project,* Freud suggests that the infant's ubiquitous experience of pain associated with and derived from the perception of the hostile object is fundamental to ego development: "There are in the first place, objects (perceptions) which make one scream because they cause pain; . . . a perception . . . emphasizes the *hostile* character of the object and serves to direct attention to the perception. Where otherwise, owing to the pain, one would have received no clear indications of the quality of the object" (p. 423).

As Freud grows disillusioned with the actual seduction theory of neurosis, he deemphasizes the importance of the role of the environment in the genesis of neurosis in favor of that played by the biologically rooted and determined development of drives. His interest focuses on the development of libido within the organizing framework of the pleasure principle. To explain masochism, he develops and relies heavily upon the concepts of destrudo, the death instinct, within the organizing framework of the constancy principle that is "beyond the pleasure principle."

In spite of his clear emphasis on energic hypotheses, Freud (1920) does offer an alternative adaptational explanation for man's irrational pursuits. This fascinating work represents a crossroads for Freud. His awareness of man's masochistic and self-destructive tendencies profoundly influences him to shift his interest from the unconscious cauldron of instinctual desires toward man's ego and its variants, miscarried in the struggle for adaptation.

Freud's (1920) deemphasized adaptational perspective provides the foundation for the formulations of this chapter. What requires emphasis is that in the corpus of Freud's work there is an almost complete lack of interest in infanticidal wishes – wishes that are possibly as ubiquitous in the unconscious as are oedipal longings. A quote from his seminal work *Inhibitions, Symptoms and Anxiety* emphasizes his stress on anxiety resulting from the ego's perception of and response to "instinctual impulses": "A wolf would probably attack us irrespectively of our behavior towards it; but the loved person would not cease to love us nor should we be threatened with castration if we did not entertain certain feelings and intentions within us. Thus such instinctual impulses are determinants of external dangers and so become dangerous in themselves" (p. 145).

The work of Berliner, Socarides, Loewenstein, and Bernstein in particular emphasize that parents experience infanticidal wishes and at moments can feel like, or as in child abuse behave like, wolves.

Masochism results from the integration of the child's narcissistic strivings with his experience of painful discomfort and perceptions of the parents as angry, sadistic, humiliating, pain-rendering, or unavailable (absent, dead, etc.).

In elaborating this formulation it is important to explore its three components. First, pain experienced as discomfort and associated with a helpless inability to relieve the resulting tension is ubiquitous in development. An object is not a necessary component of this experience. Freud (1924) in his elaboration of erotogenic masochism suggests that such experiences are prepsychological and that by eliciting a "libidinal sympathetic excitation when there is tension due to pain and unpleasure" (p. 163), they provide a "physiologic foundation" (p. 163) for psychological masochism. Second, the young child perceives the maternal (primary caretaking) object as enraged and sadistic. This perception is a profound narcissistic injury. An important question in elaborating the primary masochistic fixation is thus, when does the young child perceive the parent as pain-rendering, angry, or sadistic? In recognition of the uncertainty of our knowledge of what the infant and toddler actually experience, and in appreciation of the fact that the awareness that the object is sadistic is a complex perception probably requiring some capacity for symbolic functioning, I will equivocate somewhat in dealing with this important question. It is probable, in agreement with Mahler's findings, that the differentiating infant in the second half of the first year of life can transiently perceive the object as pain rendering. It is also probable that by the end of the second year (corresponding to the diminution of the rapprochement struggle with its characteristic corollaries of language and symbolic function development [Mahler et al., 1975, p. 101], the toddler is aware of a complex of parental responses, including anger and sadism. It is also likely that the more angry and sadistic the parent, the more difficult and distorted are these developmental processes and the resulting disturbances of development (Mahler, 1971). Complicating the situation further is the fact that certain infants are born with birth defects, neurophysiological disturbances, or "basic cores" (Weil, 1970)–factors that ensure more pain and make mother-infant synchrony more difficult to achieve. Such failures of synchrony also evoke parental disappointment, rage, sadism, and infanticidal wishes, as well as defenses against these difficult thoughts and feelings.

The third component in this formulation is the *narcissistic solution.* This defensive, representational configuration is synchronous with the developing stability of the self-representation, which roughly correlates with the rapprochement crisis and the beginnings of its resolution. By the middle of the second year of life the toddler will have great difficulty avoiding the perception of discomfort associated with limits and the particular tension that results from the perception of parents as angry and sadistic. The toddler avoids the ubiquitous narcissistic injury implicit in the perception of painful limits by attributing the inevitability of limits to the frustrating nature of the object. If the toddler can control the angry, sadistic object, not only can that threatening perception be nullified, but the more disorganizing perception of objectless, painful tension can be denied by its anthropomorphization.

Loewenstein's (1957) description of "seduction of the aggressor" is one such narcissistic solution. However, as Bergler, in elaborating Freud's (1914) concept of the genesis of the ego ideal, emphasizes, the ego's formation of the preoedipal superego via oral incorporation of the object is the more fundamental event. In addition to this introjection, a regression in integration (a splitting) of the self-representation is required to complete the narcissistic defensive process. The narcissistically invested self-representation-as-agent identifies with the narcissistically invested sadistic superego introject and imposes the pain on the self-representation-as-object. The resulting ubiquitous sado-narcissistic identification with the aggressor, structured as a ubiquitous introject in the superego, assures the perpetuation and repetition of masochism in the "character" of the ego. Freud (1917a) alludes to this splitting process in his explication of suicide in melancholia: "The analysis of melancholia now shows that *the ego can. . . treat itself as an object*" (p. 252, emphasis added).

To facilitate an exploration of the overdetermined nature of masochistic phenomena, a number of questions can be explored: What is the nature of the masochistic pleasure experience? What roles do constitutional factors play in the genesis of masochism? What is the primary masochistic fixation? What is the relative importance of preoedipal and oedipal factors in the genesis of masochism? What is the nature of conflict in general and of guilt in particular in relationship to masochistic experiences? What is the relationship of masochism to narcissism, depression, paranoia, and psychosis? What distinctions can be drawn between masochism, self-destructiveness, an unconscious need for punishment, success neurosis, and negative therapeutic reaction? What heuristic value derives from the distinction between a masochistic character and a masochistic defense, regression, and resistance?

What is the nature of the masochistic pleasure experience?

Masochism is defined as the subject's experience of pleasure in pain or in the pain of humiliating oneself or in the act of submission. This chapter explains the nature of the pleasure as deriving from three aspects of its representational context.

First, by virtue of the splitting of the self-representation, the sado-narcissistically invested self-representation-as-agent is identified with the narcissistically invested sadistic object representation structured as a superego introject. This identificatory process underlies the pleasurable experience associated with the transient restoration of the illusion of narcissistic perfection for the self-representation-as-agent. Implicit in this process is the pleasure of the seduction, defiance, or control of the superego introject. Second, the subject involved in the experience enjoys the illusion of the *presence* of the sadistic superego introject momentarily satisfied, therefore potentially satisfying. Third, the narcissistically invested self-representation-as-agent (the "I") in imposing the injury to the self-representation-as-object is often simultaneously imposing pain upon a fantasy of the disappointing, frustrating parental object that has been internalized into the self-representation-as-object via identification. This internalization is strikingly different from the introjection of the parent into the developing sadistic superego with which the narcissistically invested self-representation-as-agent identifies. Finally there is the pleasure associated with the expression of feelings of hate and love (the discharge of destrudo and libido) under the auspices of the ego, with its resulting tension reduction. In addition there is often the awareness of the absence of serious realistic damage to the subject or its important objects.

What roles do constitutional factors play in the genesis of masochism?

Freud's formulations concerning the genesis of masochism rested heavily on biological hypotheses. Although experiments with chicks and monkeys suggest that these animals may be born with a preprogrammed penchant to cling more tenaciously to the pain-rendering object (Sacks and Miller, 1975), I do not feel that the present state of knowledge permits an integration of the effects of hypothesized inborn, biologically determined predispositions to masochism into our psychological formulations on the subject. Reliance on such formulations can encourage resistance to the remembering and working through of painful and frightening memories from all levels of development that have been defended against with masochistic problem-solving modes.

The analyst may be able to recover data relating to the psychological effects of early ego impairments and the resulting disturbances in the mother-infant relationship. The effects of these difficulties are often an aspect of the family mythology, and examples of these disturbances may be recoverable in photo albums and home movies. Such data offer the contemporary analyst invaluable records of subtle parental attitudes and responses, data not available to Freud. In addition, these records may provide data concerning the analysand's earliest responses to parents as well as some sense of the subject's "basic core." Analysands report tales of how difficult they were as infants, tales that reflect their internalization of parental attitudes and solutions to their experience of the infant as frustrating and disappointing. These stories and screen memories dealing with overdetermined memories of parents as sadistic may be productively employed in formulating constructions.

What is the primary masochistic fixation?

Fleming (1975) suggests that "a self-image begins as a reflection of the affect in the mother's face" (p. 754). The developing infant and toddler has the task of integrating perceptions of a variety of maternal facial expressions and their affective connotations. As the work of Berliner and others has emphasized, the developing masochist is confronted with a mother who is more often angry and sadistic than his healthier counterpart. Because most if not all mothers and fathers are angry or sadistic toward their children at moments during the offsprings' development, the developing infant has the ubiquitous challenge of assimilating such perceptions. The primary masochistic fixation, however, does not occur until the developing self-representation is sufficiently stable and is associated with the developing ego's ability to experience an "I" and a "me." These developments are required before the ego can employ the splitting process, a fundamental component of the narcissistic solution, as a basis of the masochistic defense. These events can be correlated with the diminution of the rapprochement struggle and with the child's pleasure in mirror play, during which he can think and often say "That's me."

What is the relative importance of preoedipal and oedipal factors in the genesis of masochism?

Freud and others have stressed the role of oedipal conflict and oedipal eroticism in this context. I am emphasizing that the primary masochistic fixation can be correlated with the diminution of the rapprochement struggle. It is important, however, to emphasize that masochistic defenses, modes of attempted conflict resolution, and character organizations may primarily derive from oedipal or even postoedipal conflict. Brenner (1959, p. 212) presents a case in which the subject's masochistic character organization is significantly influenced by terrifying, shockingly traumatic real-object losses that had occurred in late adolescence and early adulthood.

The analysis and working through of masochistic defenses is characterized by the analysand's mourning the pain-rendering sadistic object and by quests for the illusion of narcissistic perfection for the self-representation-as-agent. Therefore, although these defenses may be a response to castration anxiety, oedipal guilt, postoedipal survivor guilt, or perceptions of trauma at any stage of life that threaten the integrity of the self-representation and which also necessitate assimilation, the relinquishment of them requires the working through of a defense the foundation of which derives from the preoedipal era. Such a working-through process invariably involves the assimilation of the resonant influences of preoedipal, oedipal, and postoedipal determinants of the masochistic defense – a process complemented by the integration of the overdetermined origins of these pursuits and ιat of the resonant influences of numerous factors in their perpetuation. What is the nature of conflict in general and of guilt in particular in relationship to masochistic experiences? Formulations that stress conflicts deriving from prohibited sexual wishes conceive of masochism as a condition that facilitates gratification by assuaging the superego. Guilt is thus ultimately a response to an illusion of the gratification of incestuous wishes. I agree with these formulations, but emphasize that aspect of the guilt which derives from gratification of the subject's sadism which is vengeful and destructive. Such conflicts and guilt can derive from sadistic wishes originating in the preoedipal, oedipal, and postoedipal developmental epochs. The masochistic subject is guilty because the masochistic fantasy or act represents a defiant, sadistic manipulation of parents internalized and elaborated as introjects within the superego. In addition, the masochistic subject is guilty because the masochistic fantasy or act reflects an expression of the subject's sadistic rage at the parents structured as identifications in the self-representation-as-object.

What is the relationship of masochism to narcissism, depression, paranoia, and psychosis? What are the representational differences and similarities between masochism and these complex clinical entities?

Cooper (1977) has stressed the ubiquitous, preoedipally derived relationship between narcissistic and masochistic phenomena. The contributions of Bergler, Bernstein, and Eidelberg stress the importance of narcissistic issues in masochism. Jacobson (1959), from an oedipal perspective, stresses "narcissistic gratifications" (p. 146). It is of interest that Kohut's (1979) patient Mr. Z, a narcissistic personality disorder, presents childhood and adult masturbation fantasies that are masochistic (pp. 3, 6). In his first analysis, Kohut explains that these are due to "preoedipal and pregenital fixations" but not to regression. In his second analysis, and from the perspective of his (1977) later work, these are understood as "disintegration products" (p. 262) of the self. I have stressed the narcissistic solution as a cornerstone of the masochistic problem-solving mode. Two additional factors require emphasis. First the narcissistic configuration is associated with internalizations, not of maternal sadism, but of maternal overvaluation. Second, narcissistic gratifications of distorted oedipal experiences evoke castration anxiety, which may result in masochistic reparation to a sadistic and vengeful superego.

In considering the relationship of masochism to depression it is striking to note that Freud has not commented on this clinically and theoretically important relationship. This is particularly interesting when one considers that Freud writes about narcissism, sadism, masochism, melancholia, and negative therapeutic reaction during the same time period. Some of his most important emendations to the *Three Essays on Sexuality* concerning masochism were written in the same year he wrote his brilliant *Mourning and Melancholia*. It is important to remember that Freud's contributions to our understanding of depression are written prior to the introduction of the concept of a primary aggressive drive and prior to the introduction of the structural hypothesis. They are written as an extension of his construct of narcissistic drive, which is itself an extension of instinct theory. His considerations are nevertheless proposed in clear, strikingly contemporary language that emphasizes an ego-psychological object-relations perspective. Freud stresses that depression results from the loss of a narcissistically invested object which is compensated for by a narcissistic identification. The ego is "cleaved" or split and "the critical activity of the ego" rages or discharges its "sadism and hate" on "the ego as altered by identification." Although the emphasis of Freud's explanation is upon preoedipal developmental interferences that predispose

the ego to pursue narcissistic objects and compensatory identifications, his comment on the critical activity of the ego
adumbrates his introduction of the superego construct as a
structure. Confusion derives, in part, from attempts to understand the relationship between depression, which most analysts consider to be the result of oral or preoedipal deprivation, and its relationship to the superego, which most analysts
think of as the "heir to the Oedipus complex."

Although no author has devoted a paper entirely to an exploration of the relationship between masochism and depression, a number of authors have stressed its importance. Gero
(1936) notes the relationship of "serious neurotic depression, . . . negative therapeutic reaction, [and] . . . masochism"
(p. 423) and understands his patients' depressions to be due to
"oral fixation[s]" (p. 439) which result from "oral trauma"
(p. 445). Their masochism is conceptualized as derivative of
oedipal conflicts.

Bernstein (1957) posits that "the dynamic formulations for
masochism are to some extent the same as those for depression" (p. 375). Berliner (1958) suggests that "moral masochism
can also be defined as the manifestation, with regard to object
relations, of a depressive character" (p. 44). Bergler (1961, p.
81) describes a patient whose depression he conceives of as a
defense that permits this particular patient to pursue the
pleasure of his psychic masochism. He notes that "masochists
frequently experience depression when the inwardly ex-
pected defeat fails to materialize" (p. 142). Olinick (1964), in an
important paper written from a preoedipal perspective, discusses the "concomitance of negativism, sadomasochism and
depression" (p. 540), as well as "narcissistic" (p. 540) defenses,
in his explications of negative therapeutic reaction. He notes
that when the negativism of his patients fails "there is a sadomasochistic rage and/or depression" (p. 545). He explicitly for-
mulates what Bergler has implied, that "masochism may be
. . . functioning as a defense against depression" (p. 545).

Finally, Olinick proposes that "sadomasochism 'projects' depression [into objects (the analyst)] and negativism 'rejects' [the object (the analyst)] depression" (p. 546).

Bergler's fascinating clinical observation of a depressive response to the frustration of anticipated masochistic gratification can be understood, in part, as a response to the loss of the illusory presence of the sadistic object and as a response to the narcissistic injury of the subject's inability to orchestrate a relationship to the sadistic superego introject.

From a representational perspective, the depressed subject feels helpless and hopeless. The subject feels hopeless of obtaining gratification from the beneficent object and without ability to elicit it actively. The depressed subject is suffering a symbolic loss of the narcissistically invested objects or a narcissistically invested aspect of the self-representation.[3] The masochistic subject is involved in a representational relationship with the narcissistically invested, sadistic superego introject. The masochistic subject becomes depressed when he experiences a loss – a loss of the real or fantasied sadistic object, a loss of a sense of being able to control the sadistic object, or a loss of the hope of converting the sadistic object to a loving, affirming object. I am emphasizing that the working-through process associated with the assimilation of defensive masochistic investments is characterized by depression because the subject is mourning the loss of narcissistically invested aspects of the self-representation, as well as of the fantasied presence of the sadistic object and of wishes in regard to that presence.

The issue of the relationship of masochism to psychosis in general and to paranoia, psychotic depression, and suicide in particular is an interesting one. Most authors would agree

---

[3] Brenner (1979) has emphasized the depression associated with the important narcissistic injury little girls experience when they can no longer maintain the illusion of possessing a penis. His work emphasizes the association of depressive affect, penis envy, and castration anxiety.

that the psychotic subject has often experienced profound disturbances in early object relations. Niederland's (1959) work delineates the profound disturbance in Schreber's father while Kohut (1960) has implied that Dr. Schreber probably had a psychotic character organization. Menaker (1953) has provocatively suggested that "in this way the masochistic ego reaction serves as a defense against a psychosis, that is, as a defense against the entire loss of the outside world, since at this level of development the mother represents the total world outside the ego" (p. 220). This is probably true of more seriously impaired subjects and may contribute to certain unfavorable analytic results. I (1982) have suggested that where defensive narcissistic, sadistic, or masochistic identifications are required to maintain the integrity of the self-representation, the subject is probably unanalyzable. Interpretation of these defenses results in dedifferentiation of the self-representation and is associated with psychotic regression rather than with the depression and mourning characteristic of more successful analytic endeavors. Such subjects may flee analysis because the prospect of significantly relinquishing their masochistic defenses evokes affects associated with imminent psychotic disorganization.

Bak (1946) suggests that paranoia can be understood as delusional masochism and has described the profound parental deprivation one subject has experienced throughout his life. In paranoia, the subject attempts to maintain or establish a representational relationship. It is derived, in part, from perceptions of the objects as profoundly disturbed, cold, harsh, rejecting, or murderously enraged. Difficulties in the subject's development involving fixation and reliance upon projective modes influence the subject's primary-process elaboration of the sadistic parental imago.

Asch (1980) notes the ubiquity of fusion fantasies in suicide. In the psychotic regression associated with such fantasies the representational boundaries required for the integration of the masochistic defense (the split in the self-representation and the integrity of the sadistic superego introject) are lost.

What distinctions can be drawn between masochism, self-destructiveness, an unconscious need for punishment, success neurosis, and negative therapeutic reaction? These descriptions of behavior are inevitably overdetermined, often with genetic roots in a variety of conflict-laden developmental events. Rigid investment in a particular theoretical perspective may influence an analyst to stress one or another developmental nodal point in constructions regarding these complex behaviors. Although masochistic gratifications are often an aspect, if not at times a central motivation, of these phenomena, other dynamics need to be stressed on occasion. I (1980a) have suggested that certain self-destructive events in the lives of narcissistic personality disorders are sometimes an incidental result of their impaired judgment and reality testing when they compulsively pursue illusions of narcissistic perfection for their self-representations.

An unconscious need for punishment, success neuroses, and negative therapeutic reaction are often correctly understood in oedipal terms. However, negative therapeutic reaction is a complex phenomenon occurring in the analytic relationship. It is overdetermined, often involving oral, anal, oedipal, postoedipal, narcissistic, and masochistic issues. Valenstein (1973) emphasizes the oral-early object relation component of these phenomena. Bernstein (1957) stresses the narcissistic defiance of the masochistic character while Freud (1917b) has delineated the contribution of anality to the character trait of defiance. Defiance may be significantly involved in negative therapeutic reaction phenomena. Comments on the oedipal determinant in negative therapeutic reaction are numerous.

It is worth mentioning a particular narcissistic countertransference which may indicate an analysand's sadomasochistic negative therapeutic reaction potential. The negative therapeutic reaction can be understood, in part, as an analysand's defiant sadistic response to the analyst for making a correct interpretation. On occasion it is also an expression of rage at the analyst for his narcissistic investment in being correct. The analysand may correctly perceive the analyst's minimal investment in being correct. The vulnerable analysand may exaggerate the degree of the analyst's investment and experience it as a recapitulation of the sadistic and narcissistic aspects of the parents' attitudes toward himself.

What heuristic value derives from the distinction between a masochistic character and a masochistic defense, regression, and resistance?

The former term reflects a reliance on masochistic defenses as the primary and predominant problem-solving mode of a subject's character. It may reflect profound early or life-long real deprivation and defend against psychosis, or it may derive significantly from the traumatic quality of oedipal or postoedipal developmental events. In any event no absolute statement concerning analyzability can be drawn from the predominance of narcissistic or masochistic problem-solving modes in a subject's character organization.

# CHAPTER 7

# The Dreamwork

*Dreams are brief, meagre and laconic in comparison with the wide range and wealth of the dream-thoughts. ... If the work of interpretation is carried further it may reveal still more thoughts concealed behind the dream.*

Sigmund Freud, *The Interpretation of Dreams*

*Our advanced technique of psychoanalysis, with its therapeutic zeal and goal-directed awareness of ever-changing transference and resistances, rarely, maybe too rarely, permits that intellectual partnership, that common curiosity between analyst and patient which would take a good-sized dream seriously enough to make it the object of a few hours' concerted analysis.*

Erik Erikson, "The Dream Specimen of Psychoanalysis"

Analysts have disagreed as to the role and value of the manifest dream in analysis since the early days of psychoanalytic discovery, when Stekel was accused of "wild analysis" for interpreting symbolic meanings for elements in the manifest dream. Disagreement derives, in part, from the fact that contemporary work with dreams is carried out within a variety of competing theoretical models that are quite different from Freud's (1900) original hypothesis. While some analysts still rely primarily on the topographic model, others employ the structural hypothesis, the psychology of the self, or some other construct for organizing the data of their work with dreams.

In this chapter, I will apply the hypotheses elaborated in this book to an exploration of the dreamwork in narcissistic and neurotic conflict, emphasizing the assimilative function of the ego in the dreamwork. The ego in its creation of dreams is conceived of as, in part, attempting to assimilate a variety of conflicts and traumatic experiences. These assimilative efforts employ a panoply of mechanisms in varying and interrelated organizations to result in the overdetermined manifest dream.

Virtually all of Freud's theoretical contributions on the dreamwork precede his introduction of the structural hypothesis. The only exception is his (1923b) emendation that legitimizes "dreams from above." The dreamwork is an aspect of the ego's functioning during sleep, and its development parallels that of the ego. Its ontogeny is a reflection of the ontogeny of the ego. Freud, in his prestructural contributions on the dreamwork, discusses a variety of ego organizations under the rubric of "functions" of the dream. The wish-fulfilling function of the dreamwork, delineated in his seminal contribution *The Interpretation of Dreams*, reflects an ego organization's employing dreamwork mechanisms of condensation, displacement, representation, and secondary revision. Freud's original emphasis is on the ego organized in pursuit of forbidden and repressed sexual gratifications. In this regard, he (1900) stresses dream displacement as "the essential portion of the dream-work" (p. 308) and defines it as "a transference and displacement of psychical intensities from elements which have high psychical value to elements of low psychical value" (p. 307). Thus, dreamwork is characterized by very significant distortion between signifier and signified. Freud's increasing clinical experience makes him aware of the complexity of conflict, compromise formation, and the dreamwork. "Punishment-dreams" (p. 557) confront him with the need to elaborate upon his concept of wish fulfillment and the dreamwork associated with it. In a 1919 emendation to the dream book, which heralds the structural hypothesis, Freud (1900) notes that "punishment-dreams indicate the possibility that the ego may have a greater share than was supposed in the construction of dreams" (p. 558) and that "their recognition means in a certain sense a new addition to the theory of dreams" (p. 557). Punishment dreams reflect a compromise formation and represent "a wish that the dreamer may be punished for a repressed and forbidden wishful impulse" (p. 577). Thus the ego functioning under the rubric of its wish fulfillment function strives to gratify forbidden childhood wishes and facilitate compromise formations.

Synchronous with his emendations to the wish-fulfilling function, in the highly speculative *Beyond the Pleasure Principle*, Freud introduces the concept of the "original function" of the dream. The original function attempts to organize traumatic states that have overwhelmed the stimulus barrier. The dreamwork associated with the original function aims to repeat the traumatic event represented visually in an attempt to assimilate it. Implicit in this work is the attempt to organize and modulate the affect associated with the traumatic experience. When this effort fails, a traumatic state or nightmare ensues.

In suggesting the concept of the narcissistic function of the dream, I am introducing a bridging concept between Freud's original and wish-fulfilling functions. The narcissistic function of the dream reflects an ego organized in pursuit of the restoration of illusions of narcissistic perfection for the self-representation-as-agent. The narcissistic function of the dream is related to the original function in that a self-representation endowed with such illusions feels invulnerable to traumatic states. The dreamwork associated with the original and narcissistic function of the dream shows less distortion between signifier and signified. Many "dreams from above" reflect the ego in its attempts to employ the original and narcissistic functions of the dream in the assimilation of narcissistic injuries of the dream day. Things are a bit more complex because such contemporary insults are invariably linked associatively to and resonate with unassimilated narcissistic injuries of childhood, thus influencing the adult response. In pursuing these childhood associations, the narcissistic function of the dream links up with the wish-fulfilling function because the fundamental narcissistic injuries of childhood are associated with the assimilation of the limits implicit in individuation and the socialization process. In this regard, psychoanalysts are particularly interested in the subject's response to the narcissistic injuries of weaning, toilet training, and oedipal-phase resolution. In addition, the ego may employ its narcissistic function in an attempt to resolve intersystemic conflict: it may attempt to restore an illusion of narcissistic perfection to the self-representation-as-agent in response to castration anxiety or any signal affect. Thus, while within the original function of the dream, the subject repeats the traumatic experience, the narcissistic function reflects efforts at a particular kind of identificatory alteration of the self-representation-as-agent. Both functions defend, in part, against the reexperience of painful tension states associated with frightening memories. The analysis and working through of these problem-solving modes often facilitates a clearer experience of conflicts concerning prohibited wishes associated with the dreamwork of the wish-fulfilling function. In this sense, it is as if the id were disguised by the traumatic effects of experience.

Freud (1900) emphasizes displacement as the dreamwork associated with attempts to facilitate wish fulfillment in response to repression. In prestructural terms, he conceptualizes the response of the ego to intersystemic conflict associated with a well-integrated superego. This is characteristic of the dreamwork of the "typical" neurotic character in his attempts to assimilate the wishes of the id and the sanctions of a relatively well-integrated superego. I (1980c) have suggested that the "typical" narcissistic personality disorder's superego is not so well integrated, is often fixated at the oedipal level of development and characterized by conflicting, archaically elaborated superego introjects prone to externalization. Castration anxiety often escalates, in the "typical" narcissistic personality disorder, to "catastrophic feelings of annihilation" (A. Reich, 1960, p. 224) and is characteristically associated with the ego defenses of externalization of superego introjects and sado-narcissistic identification with the fantasied imagos of the sadistic idealized superego. These latter defensive, identificatory vicissitudes are associated with the narcissistic function of the dreamwork. When these sado-narcissistic defenses are significantly worked through, masochistic identificatory defenses associated with "seduction of the aggressor" (Loewenstein, 1957) may become operative in the ego's attempts to assimilate sadistic superego introjects and may be demonstrable in the dreamwork. Assimilation of sadistic superego introjects and intrasystemic superego conflict is associated with increasing superego structuralization, diminished externalization, and the emergence of dreamwork characterized by displacement and condensation.

While gratifications associated with the narcissistic function are in and of themselves wish fulfillments, they are also employed by the ego in the dreamwork as defensive identificatory responses to the threat of a traumatic state and therefore are closely associated with its original function. The phrase "threat of a traumatic state" derives from a conception of an energic overload of a stimulus barrier. However, from a representational perspective, such a state may be understood to derive from a menacing, sadistic, archaically elaborated superego introject and "catastrophic feelings of annihilation." The narcissistic function of the dreamwork in providing gratification and in defending against traumatic states and the unconscious fantasied imagos with which such states are not infrequently associated forms a bridge in the ontogeny of the dreamwork.

Because regression in response to intersystemic conflict and postoedipal traumatic experience can evoke traumatic states, the narcissistic function is often encountered in the dreamwork associated with the ego's efforts to assimilate these experiences. In a sense the narcissistic function of the dreamwork forms a "bridge," or resonant link, between dreams "from above" and dreams "from below." It is possible that most, if not all, dreams are complex, hierarchically organized creations. When Freud speaks of dreams "from above" he refers to an aspect of a dream and the dreamwork that the analyst chooses to focus upon interpretively at a moment in an analytic process. Additional associations to such a dream might reveal other more complex aspects of the dreamwork conceptualized here under the rubric of the narcissistic and wish-fulfilling functions as well as more repressed elements "from below."

Although this chapter attempts to demonstrate the heuristic advantages of the various functions of the dreamwork being described it also suggests that such explications contribute to the redefinition of the terms *manifest* and *latent content* within the structural hypothesis, a process that has already been significantly influenced by the contributions of Waelder (1936), Erikson (1954), and Arlow and Brenner (1964).

It is a secondary premise of the chapter that the different emphases on the value of the manifest dream derive, in part, from various analysts' emphases on one or another aspect of the dreamwork. The "typical" narcissistic personality disorder is quite sensitive to narcissistic injury. Because such an injury is frequently elaborated as a mortification and may be experienced as a traumatic state, it is often appropriate, particularly early in an analysis, to emphasize the dreamwork associated with the original or narcissistic functions of the dream. Such dreams are frequently interpreted "from above." At later phases of such analyses, when the analysands' integrative and synthetic functions have been strengthened and developed to better withstand the threat of regression evoked by narcissistic injuries and anticipated traumatic states, it becomes more possible to focus on the wish-fulfilling function of their dreams. Such efforts are characterized by the pursuit of more latent content via the circuitous and creative paths Freud has described.

After exploring the relevance of this conceptual framework for clarification of the differences concerning the value of the manifest dream, I will present dreams from different phases of the analyses of two narcissistic personality disorders to highlight the complex hierarchical organization of their dreams and the relevance of the various functions of their dreamwork.

In recent years there has been an increased interest in and emphasis upon the value of the manifest content. This interest has been reinforced by increasing knowledge of the physiology of dreaming (Dement, 1960; Fisher, 1965; Hartmann, 1967), by attempts to integrate theoretical perspectives of other disciplines (Peterfreund, 1971; Polumbo, 1976; and Edelson, 1972), and in response to analytic data derived from "the widening scope of psychoanalysis" (Stone, 1954). Nevertheless, significant differences of opinion still exist as to the role and value of the manifest content of the dream in dream analysis.

It is characteristic of much of the literature on the manifest dream that contributors intent on making their point, subtly or not so subtly, encourage an either/or polemical perspective toward the value of the manifest dream that mitigates an appreciation of the complexity and hierarchical organization of the dreamwork involved in creating the manifest dream.

In his attempt to delineate the meaning of Freud's terms and concepts, Nagera (1969) defines the manifest content exactly as Freud did in 1900:

> Freud (1900) made it quite clear that his 'theory of dreams is not based on a consideration of the manifest content in dreams but refers to the thoughts which are shown by the work of interpretation to lie behind dreams' [p. 13]. He continued, 'We must make a contrast between the manifest and the latent content of dreams' [p. 643]. The above considerations and those pertaining to the *dream-work* are in fact the essential aspects of his theory [p. 54].

Nagera (1969) quotes Freud's (1916a) *Introductory Lectures* to emphasize this perspective: "'It is from these latent dream thoughts and not from a dream's manifest content that we disentangle its meaning' (p. 277)" (p. 54).

At various panels on dream analysis authorities have usually agreed with Nagera's view of the manifest content. Rangell (1956) states, "Analysis of the manifest content *alone* falls into the danger of its becoming a projective test to the 'interpreter.'. . . Most dreams from their manifest content alone cannot be understood" (p. 128). Similarly in reporting a more recent panel on the manifest content, Babcock (1966) quotes Altman as follows: "Most misunderstandings about the dream arose from the failure to make the dynamic distinction between manifest content and latent thoughts" (p. 157). In a similar vein Stein (1979) has characterized Kohut's (1977) description of "self-state dreams" (p. 108) as "anagogic" (p. 675) and has criticized his interpretation of the manifest content of these dreams: "There is no evidence that patients suffering from narcissistic personality disorders are any less complicated than other individuals – perhaps the reverse. The claim that they have different kinds of dreams, frequently if not invariably, is difficult to substantiate. Is it not possible that the resistance of the dreamer makes it far more difficult to discover the latent content?" (p. 675).

Conversely, other analysts have upheld the value of the manifest content of the dream. The Kris Study Group monograph *The Manifest Content of the Dream* (Fine et al., 1969) stresses its value in the reconstruction of traumatic events of childhood, in traumatic dreams, in recovering masturbation fantasies, and in evaluating the synthetic function and ego organization of analysands. In that monograph, Stewart (1969) emphasizes the value of the manifest content of the dream in traumatic dreams, suggesting that Freud's investment in his discovery of the unconscious biased his view of the value of the manifest content:

> The analogy of entrepreneur and capitalist which Freud used may reflect his bias in favor of the forces of the unconscious, since this was the 'new fact' of which he was the discoverer. ... Because of this 'bias' he tended to limit the function of the dreamwork to the role of camouflaging forbidden instinctual wishes, compared the manifest dream to the facade of an Italian church, and dismissed it as an 'illusion.'... This attitude toward the manifest dream seems to be a historical remnant from the early days of psychoanalysis, and predates the period of ego psychology and the structural hypothesis. In the early years understanding was limited by the topographic hypothesis in which only the concepts Ucs, Pcs and Cs were available and the model for defense was repression [pp. 85–86].

Spanjaard (1969) places an even greater emphasis on the value of the manifest content in daily analytic work. His perspective offers a radical alternative to Freud's (1900) original point of view. He stresses a *dynamic* perspective: "My thesis is that the manifest dream content usually has a subjectively conflictual aspect, and that this aspect offers us the opportunity to evaluate the most superficial layer of the conflict and thus to arrive at a construction of the potentially most useful interpretation" (p. 224).

Recently Kohut (1977), from the theoretical perspective of "the psychology of the self," has described a dream typical of narcissistic personality disorders, the analysis of which derives entirely from the analyst's response to the manifest content:

> Basically there exist two types of dreams: those expressing verbalizable latent contents (drive wishes, conflicts, and at-

tempted conflict solutions) and those attempting, with the aid of verbalizable dream-imagery, to bind the nonverbal tensions of traumatic states (the dread of overstimulation, or of the disintegration of the self [psychosis]). . . . I call these dreams "*self-state dreams.*". . . Associations to these dreams [do] not lead to any deeper understanding. . . . The correct interpretation – not a supportive psychotherapeutic maneuver – explains the dream on the basis of the analyst's knowledge of the vulnerabilities of his patient in general [pp. 108–110].

Before proceeding further it seems reasonable to digress and return to the source of our views of dream analysis. *The Interpretation of Dreams* is a text in the art and theory of dream analysis. In Chapter 7, Freud proposes that dreams exist to express infantile wishes: "*A wish which is represented in a dream must be an infantile one*" (p. 553). The psychological wish is defined in energic terms: "A current of this kind in the apparatus, starting from unpleasure and aiming at pleasure, we have termed a 'wish.' . . . Only a wish is able to set the apparatus in motion" (p. 598). Problems of current reality are incapable of initiating a dream: "My supposition is that a conscious wish can only become a dream-instigator if it succeeds in awakening an unconscious wish with the same tenor and in obtaining reinforcement from it" (p. 553). From this perspective Freud develops the topographic model of the mind. Quanta of energy associated with childhood wishes are the latent contents. These, with the aid of the dreamwork, evade the censorship and cathect preconscious thoughts and unimportant serendipitously selected events of current reality that are organized to become the manifest content.

Freud's increasing clinical experience in general and his struggle to understand man's penchant for activities "beyond the pleasure principle" influence him to reconsider his view of the human situation. His reformulations result in a model of the mind that places greater emphasis on adaptation, conflict, and the interminability of irrational investments and of the analytic process. These reformations are reflected in a shift of emphasis toward the value of the manifest content in his view of dream analysis. Freud (1911b) attempts to shift the emphasis of dream analysis as an art in itself to dream analysis as part of an ongoing analytic process: "Dream interpretation should not be pursued in analytic treatment as an art for its own sake, but . . . its handling should be subject to those technical rules that govern the conduct of the treatment as a whole" (p. 94). In this context the analysis of a dream is always incomplete: "One must be content if the attempt at interpretation brings a single pathologic wishful impulse to light" (p. 93).

In 1920, in an energic metaphor and without the terminology of a developed structural hypothesis, Freud discusses dreams of an ego unprepared for or overwhelmed by a traumatic stimulus. He proposes that the dreams of a subject with a traumatic neurosis "are endeavoring to master the stimulus retrospectively" (p. 32). They function "with a view to the psychical binding of traumatic impressions [and] obey the compulsion to repeat" (p. 33) rather than the pleasure principle: "It is impossible to classify as wish fulfillments the dreams . . . which occur in traumatic neurosis, or the dreams during psychoanalysis which bring to memory the psychical traumas of childhood" (p. 32). He notes that "if there is a 'beyond the pleasure principle' it is only consistent to grant that there was also a time before the purpose of dreams was the fulfillment of wishes" (p. 33). He goes on to suggest that the *original* function" (p. 33) of dreams is an attempt "to master the [traumatic] stimulus retrospectively" (p. 32).

Wish fulfillment in accordance with the pleasure principle is a later acquisition of a more developed ego organization. At the time of his publication of *The Ego and the Id,* Freud (1923b) alters his theory of dream formation and acknowledges that dreams can significantly derive from problems of current-day reality. These "dreams from above" (p. 111) are derived in part from "thoughts or intensions of the day before" (p. 111).

Nunberg (1932) emphasizes the "original function" of dreams: "Many dreams repeat in an undisguised form a traumatic experience, frequently one of early childhood. . . . The function of such dreams is abreaction of the trauma through reliving it over and over again" (p. 25).

Waelder (1936), from an adaptational perspective, extends these additions to the theory of dream formation and dream interpretation: "The dream phenomena can also be explained through the principle of multiple function. Every occurrence in the dream appears then likewise in eightfold function or clearly in eight groups of meaning" (p. 59). Thus a dream represents a synthesis of multiple strivings. It can derive from problems emanating from "the outerworld," from "the compulsion to repeat," from "the id," from "the superego" (p. 48), or from the subject's efforts to "assimilate" any or all of these influences. He defines "character" as representing "specific methods" of problem solving (p. 55). For Waelder the emphasis in psychic life in general and in dream formation in particular is adaptational. It is predicated upon the ego's characteristic "activity" in problem solving (p. 47).

From a similar adaptational perspective Erikson (1954) revisits Freud's landmark Irma dream. He places an original emphasis on the manifest content of the dream that has not been sufficiently appreciated. There is a "concern with form that . . . has given new depth to the surface" (p. 16). In providing a framework to elaborate, organize, and dissect a dream, Erikson from an ego-psychological perspective, suggests that the manifest dream is comprised of "configurations" (p. 18). The multiplicity of variables present in the manifest configuration transcends any one listener's capacities. Further, manifest and latent elements of a dream are not separate but exist on a continuum: "The radical differentiation between a manifest and latent dream while necessary as a means of localizing what is 'most latent' diffuses in a complicated continuum of more manifest and more latent items" (p. 34).

He provides a framework for organizing the data of the "manifest configuration" under "verbal, sensory, spatial, temporal, somatic, and object relations" and links these to the more latent dream material that consists of numerous factors including "acute life conflicts, dominant transference conflicts, repetitive conflicts and associated basic childhood conflicts" (pp. 22–23).

Erikson's term "manifest configuration" emphasizes the complexity of the manifest dream and presages the emphasis on the complexity of organization of the dreamwork that I am stressing in this chapter. It is possible that Erikson's ego-psychological term "manifest configuration" has not gained wider acceptance because many analysts share what Stewart calls Freud's biased investment in the topographic theory as an organizing framework for the interpretation of dreams. In Chapter 1 of this book I explore an aspect of this bias. To the degree that Freud and his theories serve as repositories for analysts' "original narcissistic perfection" (Freud, 1914, p. 94), their views may be "biased." Freud's (1900) historic, revolutionary, and seminal work, *The Interpretation of Dreams*, is part of all analysts' heritage. As such its concepts and terms are most valent for narcissistic investment. From the perspective of a historian of science, Sulloway (1979) has commented on the interminability of these narcissistic investments. He suggests that the mythologizing of Freud by "the Freudians . . . in many respects . . . will always be with them" (p. 503). He may be correct. In Chapter 1 I have suggested an alternative: to the degree analysts diminish their narcissistic investment of Freud and his theories, they enhance their ability to appreciate, evaluate, and elaborate his brilliant and inevitably imperfect efficacy.

Arlow and Brenner's (1964) work makes a significant contribution to this evolutionary process. They point out that although Freud (1923b) disavows the topographic theory, "most analysts would maintain (1) that the topographic theory is admiringly adapted to an explanation of the psychology of dreaming, (2) that it is clearly superior to the structural theory in this area" (p. 115). Gedo and Goldberg's (1973) concept of "theoretical complementarity" (p. 4) reflects the perspective of which Arlow and Brenner are critical. They propose that various models of the mind are best suited for organizing particular kinds of data, and suggest that "Freud's topographic approach of 1900 seems adequate for the elucidation of successful dreams. . . . The tripartite model of *The Ego and the Id* . . . best explains phenomena produced by unconscious ego and superego conflicts" (p. 18).

Arlow and Brenner's 1964 book delineates the heuristic advantage of the structural hypothesis. They emphasize that the "complete" or "total" distinction between the primary and secondary processes derives from the fact that the two "are conceived of by the topographic theory to be qualitatively distinct, rather than the *extremes of a continuous spectrum*" (p. 119, emphasis added). In analogous fashion and echoing Erikson's (1954) seminal paper, as analysts shift to the structural theory, the terms *manifest* and *latent content,* conceived of by Freud from the perspective of the topographic theory as the organizing framework for all analytic data, should be conceived as "extremes of a continuous spectrum." From this perspective, Arlow and Brenner (1964) elaborate Erikson's emphasis on the *form* of the manifest dream: "Sequences and other formal characteristics of the manifest dream do not always result from secondary revision. They may, at times, be determined primarily by the latent content of the dream. For example, a repetition of an image may signify emphasis, or the fact that a dream is in three parts may be due to the fact that the repressed wishes from which it stemmed were phallic ones" (p. 118).

From the perspective of the structural hypothesis, Erikson's term *manifest configuration* emphasizes the spectrum quality of dream content. The analyst never interprets the manifest content *alone*. This is an impossibility. The dream is a product of the analysand's mind that is a communication within the configuration of the subject's life in general and the analytic process in particular. The analyst responds to the manifest dream within the context of all the previous associations of the analytic relationship and selects an interpretation that aims at clarifying one or another aspect of that configuration. A particular communication of the analyst may fall along a spectrum from clarification of a current life situation to transference interpretation that touches the core of the infantile neurosis; that is, it may work with material that falls along a spectrum from the more descriptively conscious and less defended to the more descriptively unconscious and more defended.

Recently De Monchaux (1978) has focused upon the "telling of a dream" to the analyst and emphasized those aspects of collaborative and transferential "action" that are part of the manifest configuration of a dream: "The temptation to yield to the simplistic idea that the latent content is waiting like 'Sleeping Beauty' for the prince's interpretive kiss to release her from the curse of resistance blocks the way to scientific curiosity about the progressive and active process of transmutation of meaning which we observe in the course of dream interpretation" (p. 445).

In the past decade a number of analysts have focused on the manifest content from a variety of original perspectives. In a series of papers, Bradlow (1971, 1973, 1974; Bradlow and Coen, 1975) has attempted to study a variety of manifest contents and correlate them with considerations of character organization and questions of analyzability. From a similar perspective Oremland (1973) and Cavenar and Nash (1976) describe the use of the manifest content in the evaluation of analysands' readiness for termination. Their work suggests, in elaboration of the formulations of the Kris monograph, that the manifest configuration of a dream may be a valuable indicator of the state of integration of an analysand's psychic structure.

From the perspective of an "information processing model," Polumbo (1976) proposes that dreaming serves an essential adaptive function in the transfer of new experience to the longterm memory system. From a semiotic perspective, Edelson (1972) defines manifest and latent content: "The dream derives its efficacy from its status as 'signifier' of what is 'signified.' The manifest dream stands for or signifies meanings (latent thoughts); meaning, in this sense of the term, is that which is signified" (p. 203). He suggests that, although "these symbolic representations or symbolic forms may be, as in dreaming and language, members of different symbolic systems" (p. 274), there is a direct symbolic relationship between manifest content as symbol and more latent abstractions (ideas) or referents (objects). Although Edelson's work makes a significant contribution to interdisciplinary communication his formulations are strikingly similar to Freud's. Freud (1900), from a contemporary semiotic perspective, describes the dreamwork as "an unconscious process of thought" (p. 281) which, he emphasizes, "may easily be different from what was perceived during purposive reflection accompanied by consciousness" (p. 281). "The dream thoughts [the latent content] and the [manifest] dream-content are presented to us like two versions of the same subject-matter in two different languages" (p. 277).

Edelson's semiotic perspective is synchronous with Kohut's (1971) correlation of manifest content with latent transference configurations:

> Anxiety dreams of falling may occur (they appear to be the observe rendition of flying fantasies); they are encountered especially in patients who are about to develop a reactivation of the grandiose self in a mirror transference. And there are early dreams in which the analysand sees himself confronted

with the task of climbing a high soaring majestic mountain and looks apprehensively at the steep path and its treacherous surface in the search for a reliable footing or a secure hold. These dreams occur especially in patients who are about to develop an idealizing transference [p. 87].

In contrast to Kohut's (1977) attempts to categorize distinctly different types of dreams, these valuable clinical vignettes and his (1971) constructions concerning their relationship to process offer interesting hypotheses that could be validated statistically.

Finally, drawing from sleep-laboratory research experience and from an ego-psychological perspective, Greenberg and Pearlman (1978) suggest that "the manifest content may often portray both the problem with which the dreamer is struggling and the nature of his efforts at coping" (p. 74) and that the manifest content "can portray, in a partially *undisguised* manner, events and issues which are central to the dreamer's current emotional concerns although the dreamer may not be aware of the fact" (p. 73).

At this point I will present dreams of two narcissistic personality disorders in order to demonstrate how the hierarchical organization of the mechanisms of their dreamwork lends a complexity to their manifest dreams.

In Chapter 4, I suggest that narcissistic personality disorders can be thought of as subjects whose personalities are organized in part "beyond the pleasure principle." In Chapter 5, from a complementary perspective, I stress that narcissistic personality disorders can be defined by the prevalence of narcissistic defenses in their character organizations. Such subjects often experience frustrations as narcissistic injuries that threaten a fantasied traumatic state. Their dreamwork, in part, reflects an effort to undo the frustrations, the narcissistic injuries, of their dream day and thereby restore an illusion of narcissistic perfection to their self-representations-as-agents. Early in the analysis, work focuses on identifying their narcissistic defenses and the casual relationships that evoke them. The employment of these mechanisms within the narcissistic function of the dreamwork is typical of these analysands and characterizes early work with their dreams. At later phases of the analysis, when their responses to narcissistic injuries are more modulated by the integrative and synthetic functions of their egos that have been strengthened by analytic work, analyst and analysand have the opportunity to experience associations to more latent narcissistic injuries and to frustrated wishes of childhood. It is important to emphasize that the narcissistic personality disorders described in this chapter have had oedipal experiences that were intensely gratifying, frightening, and disappointing and that remain unresolved. The frustrations and narcissistic injuries of their daily lives often evoke memories of oedipal disappointments that are experienced as profound narcissistic injuries evocative of "catastrophic feelings of annihilation" (A. Reich, 1960, p. 224) rather than just as castration anxiety or superego anxiety. I am emphasizing, however, that it is characteristic of work early in the analysis to more frequently interpret dreams "from above" focusing on the narcissistic function of their dreamwork in its effort to assimilate the narcissistic injuries of their current reality.

Mr. S, a fifty-one-year-old married businessman and the father of two late adolescents had been in treatment (once-a-week individual psychotherapy, complemented by once-a-week group therapy with the same therapist) for three and a half years. This treatment had not "solved" his problems. He had been involved with two women, his wife and a paramour, for twelve years. The second relationship began after his wife developed a mild chronic illness which made her more needy than need satisfying. For a while Mr. S was able to avoid his guilt by believing his mistress did not exist when he was not with her. Conflict ensued and intensified in response to his mistress's greater comfort with sex as well as her interest in sharing a panoply of his interests which were of no value to his wife and which she had denigrated for many years. He thought of leaving his wife but could not tolerate the guilt and anxiety he experienced when he contemplated such an action. His parents had divorced, and he could not conceive of doing to his wife and children what his mother had done to him. Simultaneously he could not conceive of losing the pleasure he experienced with his mistress. He experienced the anticipated loss as a narcissistic injury equivalent to annihilation. He expressed this metaphorically by comparing leaving her to having a lobotomy.

After a consultation he began analysis. In the thirteenth session he talked of the pain he feared experiencing if he left his family. He fantasied that his daughter would never speak to him if he left. This fantasy created a situation in which his daughter would in essence leave him for leaving her. His fantasy indicated a connection between his current activities and his oedipal experience – an experience characterized by fantasied gratifications associated with his mother's excessive narcissistic investment in him and by significant disappointments associated with his parents' divorce in his late latency. Mr. S's oedipal experience had other characteristics not infrequently observed in narcissistic personality disorders (see Rothstein, 1979b). In association to the fantasy of leaving his family for a life with his mistress, he related the following dream: "I was taking her to my house to show her how nice it was. My wife and the kids were sleeping in the same bed." He associated his pleasurable feeling in the dream of being with his mistress and of seeing his wife and the kids safe and happy. The analyst focused upon the dream "from above" and Mr. S's ego's efforts to assimilate the frustrations of his current reality experienced as a narcissistic injury. By creating a manifest dream in which he could keep his mistress and avoid guilt. Mr.

S's dream performed a narcissistic function by creating the illusion that limits and the pain of conflict could be avoided. The analyst interpreted that the dream gratified his wish to avoid the guilt associated with the fantasy of hurting his family and the pain of losing his mistress. At this early phase in the analysis, no attempt was made to deepen his appreciation of his subjective experience of frustration, his fear of his murderous rage, the relationship between his current situation and the traumatic memories of his childhood, their oedipal implications, or the defensive identifications and narcissistic investments they motivated. However, in response to the analyst's interpretation, he reported two terrifying recurrent childhood dreams. In the first he described a family of snakes. They lived in the basement and lured his father, who was not smart enough to avoid them, away from home; sometimes his mother, too. In the second dream, he was sleeping in his parents' bedroom rather than next to it. He would wake up and see a man climbing through the window to stab his father. He would scream and wake up terrified. Although oedipal elements "from below" are clear in both the manifest dream and associations to it, at this very early stage in the work it seemed more appropriate to interpret the dream "from above" in relationship to the realistic turmoil of Mr. S's current reality.

Tolstoy (1878) brilliantly portrays Anna Karenina's struggle to resolve a similar narcissistic conflict in a manifest dream strikingly similar in form to the dream Mr. S reported.

Anna wished to avoid the spectrum of painful fantasies associated with the experience of conflict. She wished to simplify life. She had a superego and felt anxious and guilty about her infidelity. She hated her husband, Aleksey Aleksandrovich, and longed for the pleasure of her lover's Aleksey Vronsky's adulation, but she perceived and empathized with Aleksandrovich's pain. The dream solved her conflict by omnipotently decreeing Anna's right to polygamy: "She dreamed that both were her husbands at once, that both were lavishing caresses on her. Aleksey Aleksandrovich was weeping, kissing her hands, and saying, "how good it is now!" and Aleksey Vronsky was there too, and *he too was her husband*. And she was amazed that it had once seemed impossible to her, was explaining to them, laughing, that *this was so much simpler* and that now both of them were happy and contented" (pp. 159–160, emphasis added).

In the third month of his analysis Mr. S began a session by reporting, "Last night I was to dinner with my mistress and another couple. We got smashed. She got sick. I was ready to make love and she was sick. I was enraged 'cause I couldn't have what I wanted when I wanted it. Then I dreamed I left the restaurant alone and took a cab to the Commodore – then I found myself in a room with her. In another part of the dream we were making love." He went on to ponder why his mistress had become ill. In response to the analyst's query concerning the Commodore, Mr. S reported that that was where he had gone yearly for a business meeting before he knew her. At this relatively early stage in the analysis, the analyst interpreted the dream "from above" and once again focused on the narcissistic function of the dreamwork, suggesting to Mr. S that the dream created the illusion of undoing his experience of frustration. This interpretation implied that in undoing frustration an illusion of narcissistic perfection had been transiently restored to the self-representation-as-agent. The analyst interpreted that the frustration of the mistress's illness was undone by first going back in time to a moment when she did not exist for him and then by curing her and restoring her to her more usual gratifying state. Mr. S responded, "In the morning she and I made love. She knew how I felt. It wouldn't have happened with my wife that way."

Mr. C, a middle-aged lawyer, was in his sixth year of analysis. In emphasizing his oedipal conflicts, I (1979b) have previously described the traumatic quality of his oedipal situation. Both parents were self involved. The mother was overtly seductive, unconsciously exposing her genitals to the boy sitting at her feet, while his father, a sportsman and hunter, was disappointing and weak. Mr. C's analytic work was characterized by chronic acting up deriving from an almost perverse attraction for extramarital sexual involvement.

His penchant for action would influence Kohut (1977) to consider him a "narcissistic behavior disorder." (p. 193) rather than a "narcissistic personality disorder" (p. 193).

In the third year of his analysis Mr. C expressed the nature of his conflict as between his longing for what Erikson (1950) terms "ego integrity" (p. 268) and his addictive attraction for the perverse: "I want to get to age seventy and look back and respect my life. I should be more interested in my daughter than in M sucking my cock – for whatever reason it makes me feel bad. I'm going to see M tonight and I don't want to."

Mr. C brought dreams in and worked on them in a productive manner. Many of the manifest contents of his dreams dealt with overt aggression as well as with undisguised sexual and grandiose longings. Occasional dreams seemed to repeat, in almost undisguised form, aspects of his traumatic childhood. Later in his analysis, occasional dreams were worked with in depth. A dream worked on in the sixth year of his analysis is reported to demonstrate the complexity of dreams of narcissistic personality disorders and the hierarchical organization of the mechanisms of their dreamwork. Mr. C worked with this dream during thirteen of sixteen sessions in a four week period. In addition, he spontaneously associated to elements of the manifest configuration of the dream during the ensuing year of the analysis.

Mr. C began the session in which he reported the dream distraught: "I can't believe it . . . . My wife is pregnant again. If I force her to have another abortion that's the end of the marriage." His wife's pregnancy evoked "catastrophic feelings of annihilation" because it threatened a number of Mr. C's narcissistically invested pursuits. These pursuits reflected, in part, overdetermined compromise formations that facilitated a panoply of fantasied, oedipally organized gratifications. These defended, in part, against remembering numerous childhood disappointments experienced as narcissistic injuries. After considering his difficult situation, Mr. C reported his dream: "I was with T, we went to the Mediterranean and were ringed by beautiful scenery that was right out of a romantic Cary Grant movie I was watching during the day. I had a gun and I was going grouse hunting" – he associated that the grouse is the perfect game bird – "and the Clint Eastwood sight on my gun (that's from another movie I was watching during the day) wouldn't work and I saw a tidal wave coming in (that reminds me of tension-filled summers I spent with my first wife), then I'm going for a car and I get out but I lose T, we're not able to get out together, but I escape."

He associated to his wife's pregnancy. He couldn't believe it was happening again. He stated, "women are the ultimate threat to my existence. They are the tidal wave. They interfere with all my pleasures." These associations reflect Mr. C's narcissistic experience of his object world – one influenced by his fantasied pursuit of illusions of narcissistic perfection for his self-representation-as-agent. This organized fantasy influenced his sense of entitlement to have a pure pleasure state and to experience the inevitable frustrations that derive from the object's separate existence as a life-threatening assault on his narcissistically invested view of himself. The awareness of his wife's pregnancy evoked overdetermined "catastrophic feelings of annihilation." These intense feelings and associated unconscious fantasies were represented in the manifest configuration by the dreamwork as "the tidal wave." He began the next two sessions by relating that he could see the tidal wave as he began the session. In the third session, in association to the tidal wave, he recaptured the frustrating experiences of being married to his first wife and of having a family with her. He recalled, "I remember how destructive she was. She insisted I mold my life around a family. I felt guilty about going to a football game. Fuck it. So other than stolen pleasures I missed the things I like to do. Without the kids and with some money I can do the things I like to do. I'm thinking of taking T or my brother to Iceland to fish for Atlantic salmon – the perfect fish. It would be a great experience." In the sixth postdream session, he saw the tidal wave again. By this time it was clear that it was a metaphor or "signifier" for his sense of annihilation anxiety in response to his wife's pregnancy. The pregnancy threatened his potential to continue to enact a number of defensive identifications that he felt to be essential to his survival and to the maintenance of the integration of illusions of narcissistic perfection in his self-representation-as-agent. If he didn't satisfy his wife, he felt she would destroy him as he felt his mother had destroyed his father. If he had a baby with his wife, he believed she would prevent him from seeking pleasures with other men; pleasures that were motivated by both fear of women and by a wish to undo his experience of rage-filled disappointment in his father. This time, however, he reported, "I see the Bell Tower at Harvard. It is going to be knocked over by a tidal wave." This additional fragment of manifest content directed his associations to a sequence of childhood memories. He stated, "The tidal wave is going to demolish my family home. We're going to sell the house. I don't want to own it with my brother and sister. I want to have my share of the money and not be subject to anyone else's control. Right now I'm feeling powerless in the firm, in the business deal, with my wife and her pregnancy, when I'm not really helpless. The tidal wave is knocking over Cambridge." Mr. C became aware that making a life with his wife would threaten his symbolic involvement with his mother and father. He noted, "I never had a real relationship with my mother anyway. She would say 'perform for me, I love my own father not yours. Your father is a shit! You're great, perform and be special for me.' That's how I stay special to my mother."

The analyst offered an interpretation emphasizing Mrs. C's pregnancy as a threat to Mr. C's narcissistically invested, oedipally organized, fantasied relationship with his mother. The analyst commented, "Everytime you perform and suck a woman's cunt you're being special to your mother. In an adult relationship disappointment is inevitable. Being special in your sense is an impossibility. To be able to enjoy having a child you have to be able to enjoy treating the young child in the way you want to be treated by your wife and your mother." Mr. C pondered these issues over the weekend and began the first session of the next week by associating to the tower: "It was my high-school days. I was king of the walk, a star . . . afraid though . . . afraid of failing and humiliation. There's Pop watching me at a football game – opening game of my senior year, new uniforms – being proud but feeling resentment. Why can't he be successful in his own right so he doesn't need my success? Why do I have to listen to Mom criticize him all the time? My own marriage to my wife is a sham marriage like my mother's and father's. Never committed, complain all the time and never leave." His associations emphasized the defensive function of his narcissistic investments in relationship to negative oedipal disappointments expressed in the screen memory of real adolescent disappointments in his father.

Later in the session his associations focused on his current investments by pursuing illusions of narcissistic perfection for his self-representation-as-agent. He noted, "I don't want to give up being special with men or women, I find it hard to be out front about it. Women want more, they want intimacy. I just want to feel special. I feel that my not accepting limits is neurotic and self-destructive. . . . I shouldn't want to pursue it. Then I'm indecisive because it seems like an inappropriate goal so I haven't pursued it all out. I'm like Peter Pan looking for a mythical fairyland. I have a time bomb ticking away" – his wife's pregnancy – "I could get out of this marriage and what have I gained? I have a number of girlfriends. . . . I just want to be special to a number of women. It doesn't sound so exciting. For me it's having to have it all and that I have to break. I'm really struggling with this."

Mr. C began the next session with: "These are hard times for me. I do like being with one woman. I just haven't come to grips with being tied to a tree." Mr. C had been literally tied to a tree by his mother to "keep him out of trouble" when he was three or four years old. "Fucking around doesn't seem so terrific. I'd miss my wife. I don't know if I could live with anyone else. I'm lonely and depressed. This half-life I've been living. When I see myself as alone, the other relationships seem less important. I become more aware I'm just chasing the beautiful cunt or the great cocksuck – it seems shallow. I see the addiction clearer now."

Mr. C began the first session of the following week by informing the analyst that his wife was staining and was going to have an abortion. He stated, "I've put my marriage in the closet and cut myself off from the normal avenues of living. I remember happy times with my wife years ago. What happened to that?"

In the year after the dream being considered was reported, work proceeded on Mr. C's narcissistic investments and their defensive relationship to unresolved preoedipal and oedipal conflicts. During that time, the tidal wave and the beautiful scenery, two elements of the manifest content of the dream, spontaneously appeared in Mr. C's associations. Excerpts from seven additional sessions in which the dream was worked with demonstrate that specific elements of the manifest content led to associations that facilitated the recovery of specific childhood memories of primal-scene trauma within the context of a distorted and intensified oedipal situation. In addition, associations to primal-scene trauma facilitated the analysis of chronic transference resistances. Finally these memories deepened Mr. C's understanding of the genesis of some of his narcissistic investments and facilitated the process of assimilating their defensive function.

Six weeks after the dream, Mr. C began a session, that followed a week's interruption due to the analyst's absence, by asking the analyst, "How are you?" The week was also noteworthy, because Mr. C was about to experience his fiftieth birthday. He noted, "Coming over I heard a woman singing and asked her, 'What right do you have to be so happy?'" The analyst identified Mr. C's envy of the analyst's and the woman's happiness. Mr. C confirmed this and lamented his unhappy state. Work proceeded from Mr. C's envy of his fantasy of the analyst's happiness to his fear of more vigorously pursuing his own happiness. Instead he had sought gratifications associated with stolen pleasures.

These quests were derived, in part, from his fear of his mother's controlling and extractive nature, as well as from his fear of his own rage at his father for being absent and weak. In addition, he had pursued symbolic positive oedipal gratifications to deny and undo the intensely felt narcissistic injuries of his formative years. These gratifications evoked fears of retaliation by a vengeful superego introject which motivated further quests for illusions of narcissistic perfection for the self-representation-as-agent. Mr. C associated to the tidal wave. He felt he would be destroyed if he committed himself to a life with his wife: "I'll be tied to a tree again. . . . It will be my first marriage all over again. I feel I can't survive without a central woman and I can't face their anger." Mr. C began his next session stating "I fear pleasure, I'm attracted to illusions of control. Rationally I know I'm in control, irrationally I see the tidal wave and the tower being knocked over."

The next session of the week coincided with Mr. C's fiftieth birthday. He focused on his rage at and disappointment in his senior associates, who did not remember his birthday. The analyst interpreted Mr. C's disappointment that the analyst had not begun the session with congratulations and noted Mr. C's wish to undo his disappointment in his father in the transference and his work relationships. In addition, it was interpreted that Mr. C was experiencing his fiftieth birthday as an oedipal victory, that the quest for paternal love, was, in part, motivated in defense against the more open pursuit of success and pleasure. The analyst commented, "Because your mother considered your father a failure and because he died before he was fifty you feel it is a crime to be alive and to achieve and be openly successful and happy." Mr. C mused that as a child he was always free to steal hidden pleasures by crawling under tables and looking up ladies' dresses but that he had panicked and fled the pleasure of a piano recital where his mother was to have publicly admired him.

In the next session, the tidal wave appeared once again in Mr. C's thoughts. His associations deepened his appreciation that for him this seemed to signify the catastrophic sense of annihilation he felt when he thought of conflict with a woman. He described feeling a "glimmer of anxiety associated with the awareness that if I commit myself to a woman it would be an infidelity to my mother." Then he reported, "I see a tidal wave, annihilation, humiliation – I see the image of setting the fire when I was three."

A tower appeared in Mr. C's associations in a number of his sessions. His associations to the tower had primal-scene significance: more specifically, it derived in part, from a humiliating and painful memory with primal-scene and oedipal meanings. Approximately five minutes after beginning a session four months after reporting the dream, Mr. C associated, "I'm thinking of a tower, I'm five years old. Mother was visiting a friend in a smoking jacket who I didn't like. [Pause] I was never happy as a child. There is a lot of pain in me I don't want to face. I was in the tower looking over the serene valley and it felt good. Mother came and got me and took me down." The analyst commented, "The pain of your current reality reminds you of the pain of your childhood. You seek lonely perfect pleasures to avoid reexperiencing the frightening and painful feelings of your childhood." Mr. C responded, "I'm thinking of salmon-fishing. I don't need D's perfect cunt anymore."

Mr. C began a session six months after the dream in question by describing his sense of humiliation at being kept waiting by the analyst. He associated, "Waiting out there I thought of the little boy in the tower. I see myself up there disappointed and enchanted by the wonderful view. Nature is my biggest realistic escape. Being with women is always contaminated by its being stolen. This guy in the smoking jacket – I didn't like him. I felt he was greasy. I didn't trust him."

These associations offer a striking example of the process of what Freud has described as "secondary narcissism," the relationship between "feeling disappointed" in the object and Mr. C's becoming "enchanted" with the scenery. In addition these associations facilitate our understanding of the genetic roots of the "beautiful scenery" element of the manifest content of the dream.

A week later Mr. C associated, "I see the tower – I'm thinking of starting a new affair." The analyst offered an incomplete primal-scene construction: "You are thinking of an affair to avoid experiencing the painful and frightening memory of having the door shut in your face by your mother while she pursued pleasures with another man – you felt humiliated." Mr. C responded, "Yes, how often I feel that with my wife." In the next session, Mr. C thought of the tower and related, "I felt humiliated by being shut out by another man I didn't like. I didn't like that guy at all. I was a powerless little kid. I felt like an insect, he didn't care about me at all. I got some surcease from the landscape. I still do that in a big way – I'm thinking of my father and his father, they were farmers – the land. After that, when I was a bit older, my father came back and he was humiliated – his life was one of abject humiliation." He paused, then remarked, "Women aren't so dangerous. I set it up to be humiliated by them. As I say that, the image that goes through my mind is of fucking someone in the ass and turning the humiliation around."

It is important to emphasize that although this dream was worked with intensively its analysis was incomplete. More sustained analysis of the dream, however, enabled Mr. C to work with the catastrophic manifest content of the dream in relationship to three interrelated areas: (1) the threatened narcissistic injury of his current life, (2) the narcissistic, sadistic, and masochistic defenses that were basic elements of his character organization, and (3) their relationship to the more latent content of the traumatic quality and conflictual nature of his preoedipal, oedipal, and postoedipal relationships with his mother and father. His wife's pregnancy, experienced as a narcissistic injury of his dream day, threatened relatively stable narcissistically invested aspects of Mr. C's character. Associations to the dream facilitated work on the assimilation of these investments and their function in defending Mr. C from remembering and reexperiencing painful and frightening negative and positive oedipal disappointments.

It is a characteristic of many narcissistic personality disorders to be extremely sensitive to frustrations in general and to the focused experience of frustration in the transference. Activity is a common defense of narcissistic personality disorders' character armor in response to frustration, while acting out is a typical resistance when such issues are experienced in the transference. Their activity derives from and reflects the enactment of a fantasy, and like any fantasy, it is overdetermined and serves multiple functions. It is an important task with action-prone narcissistic personality disorders to help them to delay acting in the service of defining the underlying fantasy and its overdetermined roots.

Mr. C's penchant for activity derived, in part, from defensive identifications intended to undo extremely painful, passively experienced narcissistic mortifications. Mr. C's defensive identifications protected him from feared experiences of overdetermined "catastrophic feelings of annihilation." His most characteristic defenses were sado-narcissistic identifications with poorly integrated superego introjects.

In-depth analysis of this dream facilitated Mr. C's understanding of the genetic roots of two tenacious action resistances. Primal-scene memories were recovered in response to being kept waiting by the analyst. Mr. C struggled with an enigmatic transference resistance; he had difficulty being on time for his hour. In the context of working on this dream, this transference resistance was better understood as a defense against a panoply of painful childhood memories, particularly his father's absence and lack of attention.

In this context, Segal's (1969) concept of "identification with the doer" (p. 486) is helpful. Mr. C does to the analyst and his wife what he feels his mother and father have done to him.

Christmas marked an increase in acting out. The analyst would often leave Mr. C at Christmas, while Mr. C would send his wife to visit her parents and engage in increased activity with paramours. Work on this dream, enabled Mr. C to assimilate some of the pain of his oedipal experiences and to tolerate these memories in consciousness for greater periods of time. Mr. C related, "All I remember of Christmas when I was five was shooting the ornaments off the tree. . . . That got his attention. They were separated but went out and left me alone. I don't remember spending any time with him, he just wasn't there. Boy was he angry when he saw the tree. That got his attention and then I was humiliated." Mr. C was able to understand his present Christmas activity as motivated, in part, by a wish to avoid the painful and frightening feelings associated with the analyst's absence, an absence that associatively revivified memories of the disappointments of his father's absence during his oedipal stage of development. More specifically, he would expiate his guilt for his sadistic acting out and get the analyst's attention as he had his father's, by relating how bad he had been while the analyst was away.

As Waelder (1930) suggests, dreams reflect characteristic assimilative problem-solving modes. Although the narcissistic problem-solving mode and the narcissistic function of the dreamwork are ubiquitous, they are the sine qua non of the character armor of the "typical" narcissistic personality disorder. Early process in analytic work with narcissistic personality disorders, in part, aims to identify and interpret the defensive function of these problem-solving aspects of character as reflected in the dreamwork. Assimilation of these modes and their defensive functions is facilitated by interpreting dreams "from above" in relationship to events of the dream day, experienced as narcissistic injuries. Then, associations, via the analysis of displacements and condensations more characteristic of the wish-fulfillment function of the dreamwork, may lead to more repressed elements derived from unresolved conflicts of early childhood in general and the oedipal phase of development in particular. Conflict is often more intensely felt by the narcissistic personality disorder because he feels entitled to be gratified, because he is unconsciously encouraged to seek consciously prohibited gratifications, and because disappointments in one or both parents leave his superego without the enforcing presences associated with the structuralizations of more normal oedipal resolution. I am suggesting, however, that narcissistic problem-solving modes employed in the dreamwork derive from, and are related to, the original function of dreams – i.e., man's repetitive compulsion to attempt to master traumatic situations. The typical narcissistic personality disorder's character organization can be conceptualized as organized, in part, "beyond the pleasure principle" in an effort to protect against the anticipated traumatic situation experienced as "annihilation" anxiety.

The "typical" narcissistic personality disorder's character derives from and defends against formative disappointments from all stages of childhood that have been experienced as *traumatic*. His sense of security derives significantly from pursuits of illusions of narcissitic perfection for the self-representation-as-agent. Conflict ensues when that investment is threatened. Such conflict may result in a panoply of intra- and intersystemic conflicts and attempted conflict resolutions, as well as in conflicts with frustrating aspects of the real world. A subject may find himself enraged at a frustrating object or part of the self experienced as an object. In Chapter 2, I conceptualize such data as reflective of the *intra*systemic conflict associated with the interminable assimilative struggle between the narcissistically invested self-representation-as-agent and the self-representation-as-agent that is organized in relationship to the reality principle. In addition, *inter*systemic conflict between the subject's narcissistically invested self-representation-as-agent and superego may result in guilt in response to exploitiveness or rage toward the frustrating object. Further intersystemtic conflict associated with anxiety and guilt ensues when the subject fails to fulfill his role as his parents' narcissistic object. Finally, guilt and castration anxiety derive from repressed oedipal longings. Such conflicts may evoke regressive anthropomorphization and externalization of superego function. Aspects of these conflicts, particularly related to pursuits of defensive narcissistic investments reflected in the narcissistic function of the dreamwork, are portrayed, sometimes in relatively undisguised form, in the manifest configuration of dreams.

The fundamental narcissistic problem-solving mode as expressed in the dreamwork is closer to what Freud refers to as the "original function" of dreaming. In Chapter 4, I suggest that the "original function" of the dreamwork derives from and reflects a problem-solving mode of the immature ego that repeats traumatic memories in "almost" undisguised form in an attempt to facilitate their active assimilation. In addition the subject's dreamwork employs a "narcissistic function" that is closely related to the "original function," that is, the subject struggles to restore a sense of the original narcissistic perfection to the self-representation-as-agent in order to create the illusion of invulnerability to the anticipated traumatic experience. The dreamwork and the typical manifest configurations of the dreams may have less distortion between signifier and signified. The "almost" undisguised nature of such dreams emphasizes their complexity. The subtle alteration in the manifest content of the original traumatic experience may represent a nodal "point" (Freud, 1900, p. 515) that indicates a potential associative link to repressed elements organized under the aegis of the "wish-fulfilling" function of the dreamwork. These can be meaningfully pursued at appropriate stages of an analysis.

An essential aspect of the analyst's task with the narcissistic personality disorder is not only to recover the repressed oedipal wishes but also to facilitate the assimilation of the painful and frightening affects associated with the traumatic experience with the often easily recoverable memories of the traumatic situation. The subject has to be helped to share the pain, anxiety, and fantasied meanings associated with the memories of traumatic experiences with the analyst in order to begin to assimilate the defensive function of narcissistic problem-solving modes. As work proceeds on narcissistic problem-solving modes, often motivated in response to current life situations that are experienced as narcissistic injuries and which threaten to evoke memories of "traumatic" states, more latent preoedipal, oedipal, and postoedipal material often emerges. This is evident in the work with Mr. S and Mr. C. The dream from Mr. S's thirteenth session is dealt with as Tolstoy dealt with Anna's dream, strictly in terms of narcissistic conflict. This is appropriate at this very early stage of Mr. S's analysis. Both of Mr. S's dreams are dealt with as dreams "from above." The frustrations of his current situation are experienced as profound life-threatening limits to the self-representation-as-agent, because they threaten character defenses derived from and associated with profoundly disturbing childhood experiences. The recall of these experiences threatens a "traumatic" state. His dreams create a fantasy that changes reality and thereby protects him from the experience of definitive limits to his narcissistically invested self-representation-as-agent. Mr. S's dreamwork fulfills a "narcissistic function" by restoring the sense of original narcissistic perfection to the self-representation. However, once the defensive narcissistic function of the dream is interpreted "from above" two childhood dreams are reported portraying the traumatic, terrifying, and gratifying nature of Mr. S's oedipal experience. Conflicts in response to oedipal wishes and parenticidal urges are obvious in the manifest content and associations to the dream reported in Mr. S's thirteenth analytic hour. A good deal of his analysis will undoubtedly focus on the assimilation of his unresolved and active oedipal conflicts.

I (1979b) have suggested that "narcissistic personality disorders . . . usually struggle with an admixture and alternation of oedipal and preoedipal issues. Both aspects need to be analyzed. Each can act as a resistance to impede the analysis of the other" (p. 189). Mr. S and Mr. C have experienced traumatic family disruptions during their oedipal phases of development. I am suggesting that these men's life experiences (both preoedipal and oedipal) have left them excessively sensitive to frustration. These factors predispose them to a variety of defensive and regressive problem-solving modes that reflected a longing for a conflict-free state. Such modes, however, are not necessarily reflective of an arrest in the development of a subject's representational world. Rather they represent defenses often mobilized by a panoply of signal affects experienced as components of intra- and intersystemic conflicts. These defenses are built of a conglomerate of representations, some of which have their origin very early in life. These narcissistic, sadistic, and masochistic defenses, problem solving modes and/or aspects of "character" have their roots in preoedipal experience. However, what is being stressed is the distinction between a true developmental arrest and a regression from oedipal and postoedipal conflict to a preoedipal fixation or mode of problem solving.

The overdetermined nature of Mr. C's tie to his parents has been emphasized. Although Mr. C's ties to his mother are importantly influenced by preoedipal factors his defined self-representation is significantly organized on an oedipal level in relationship to conflicting parental representations structured within his ego ideal and supergo. Mr. C's superego has intensely active fixations at the oedipal stage of development. His superego lacks the enforcing presence that derives from the introjection of the respected, admirable paternal image associated with a more normal resolution of the oedipal stage of development. In addition oedipal maternal superego introjects prohibit and encourage fantasies of oedipal conquest. Castration anxiety associated with prohibited oedipal wishes and annihilation anxiety associated with conflict over matricidal rage in response to the experience of oedipal humiliations evoke regressive quests for the restoration of illusions of narcissistic perfection for the self-representation-as-agent. Manifestations of these pursuits are observed in Mr. C's fantasies and behavior and in the narcissistic function of his dreamwork.

In attempting to communicate the quality of these subjects' life experiences I have become impressed with the difficulty of writing about one or another factor of their experiences. Although the process is heuristically beneficial, something is lost of the overdetermined nature of their lives. When considering a similar issue in relationship to the overdetermined nature of the genesis of the character trait of defiance, Freud (1917b) implies that defiance develops at the anal stage of development, in part, as a narcissistic defense against the narcissistic injury of the perception of disappointment in the parental object. Freud notes that "its feces are the infant's first gift, a part of his body which he will give up only on persuasion by someone he loves . . . as a token of affection; for as a rule, infants do not dirty strangers. . . . He either . . . sacrifices his feces . . . or else retains them . . . as a means of asserting his will. If he makes the latter choice we are in the presence of defiance (obstinacy) which . . . springs from a narcissistic clinging to anal eroticism" (p. 130).

In a similar manner, many narcissistic personality disorders are angry at and disappointed in their parents. They are terrified by their feelings and obstinately refuse to accept the mortifying nature of their oedipal experience. In defense against assimilating these painful and frightening disappointments they pursue narcissistic, sadistic, and masochistic defenses and suffer from a narcissistic, sadistic, and masochistic clinging to oedipal eroticism. Their oedipal situations have been both intensely gratifying, frightening, and disappointing. Oedipal conflicts are unresolved and remain active as organizers of these subjects' feelings and behavior. They have not been able to mourn (in Blos's [1962] meaning of the term) their parents sufficiently to be able to tolerate and enjoy life with another adult. Their narcissistically, sadistically, and masochistically invested character organizations attempt to maintain their oedipal gratifications while defending against recapitulations of oedipal disappointments experienced as traumatic narcissistic injuries, as well as against anticipated dangers.

Their dreams reflect the overdetermined, hierarchically organized nature of their conflicts. Their egos often employ the original, the narcissistic, and the wish-fulfilling functions in their dreamwork. Early in their analyses, work often

focuses upon the utilization of narcissistically invested problem-solving attempts to resolve threats to the integration of
their investments of narcissistic perfection in their self-
representations. Failure at such assimilative efforts threatens
a "traumatic" state. The manifest content of such dreams
reflects the "original" and narcissistic functions of dreams
and, from this perspective, is characterized by minimal or only
modest distortion between signifier and signified. Nevertheless, as Mr. S's and Mr. C's dreams demonstrate, our patients'
minds are complex. The narcissistically invested, problem-
solving, assimilative efforts of their dreamwork that are often
easily discernible in their manifest dreams are invariably linked
associatively to more latent and repressed preoedipal,
oedipal, and postoedipal themes elaborated by mechanisms of
the dreamwork associated with its wish-fulfilling function.
The multiplicity of their modes of problem solving and of the
functions of their dreamwork need to be analyzed and assimilated.

# Conclusion

In concluding this book, I feel momentarily satisfied but profoundly aware of its inevitable incompleteness. From an evolutionary perspective that is as it should be. Major areas of ego development and functioning await further explication. The theory of affects, learning, and cognitive and symbolic development are just some of the areas of ego psychology that require attention. These emendations will undoubtedly be enriched by the rapidly increasing developmental data of infant observation.

In the introduction to this book, I note my interest in elaborating Waelder's work on overdetermination and his concept of assimilation. The emphasis of his work is on the temporal perspective of the ego's here-and-now adaptational struggle to assimilate multiple demands upon it from the id, from the superego, from the external world, and from the compulsion to repeat. Implicit in Waelder is his appreciation of the interminable assimilative struggle of the self-representation-as-agent that is organized in relation to reality to assimilate the influence of the past on the here and now.

Waelder's emphasis is on the complexity and creativity of human experience. His elaboration of the assimilative struggle of the ego in the face of multiple influences mitigates the sometimes simplistic contributions of others who stress one factor to the seeming exclusion of others. Similarly his contribution counters the either/or polemics that characterize many discussions between proponents of competing theories.

An either/or perspective on such issues as the influence of

preoedipal versus oedipal factors, nature versus nurture, and drive derivatives versus the role of the real object and trauma on character development, on the dreamwork, on symptom formation, and on the analytic process itself is an oversimplification that does not do justice to the complexity of human experience. It is a premise of the first chapter of this book that an either/or perspective derives, in part, from revolutionary competition between paradigm proponents. Such a perspective leads to statements such as "I'm right, you're wrong." On the other hand, an evolutionary perspective facilitates the kind of thinking that allows emphasis of a previously deemphasized or neglected aspect of experience. It thereby contributes to our increasing appreciation and understanding of the complexity of the human situation.

There is a *resonance* between past and present, between various stages of development, as well as between drive derivatives and the influence of the real object internalized as psychic structure that makes unifactorial emphases and explanations unsatisfactory. Analysts and analysands are left with the realistic, and interminable, task of struggling to assimilate these influences as they resonate on their present experience. The pursuit of such an effort affords the self-representation-as-agent that is organized in relationship to the reality testing, judgment, and the integrative functions of the ego a greater chance to assimilate the interminable irrational influences from within, the exigencies of life from without, and finally one's own vulnerability and finiteness.

# References

Alexander, F. (1929), The need for punishment and the death instinct. *Internat. J. Psycho-Anal.*, 10:256–267.

———— & French, T. (1948), The principle of corrective emotional experience – the case of Jean Valjean. In: *Psychoanalytic Theory: Principles and Application.* New York: Roland, pp. 66–70.

Andreas-Salomé, L. (1921), The dual orientation of narcissism. *Psychoanal. Quart.*, 1961, 30:1–30.

Arlow, J. (1956), In report on the panel on the problem of masochism in the theory and technique of psychoanalysis. *J. Amer. Psychoanal. Assn.*, 4:526–538.

———— (1980), The revenge motive in the primal scene. *J. Amer. Psychoanal. Assn.*, 28:518–541.

———— & Brenner, C. (1964), *Psychoanalytic Concepts and the Structural Theory.* New York: International Universities Press.

Asch, S. (1980), Suicide and the hidden executioner. *Internat. Rev. Psycho-Anal.*, 7:51–60.

Babcock, C. (1966), The manifest content of the dream. *J. Amer. Psychoanal. Assn.*, 14:154–171.

Bak, R. (1946), Masochism in paranoia. *Psychoanal. Quart.*, 15:285–301.

Basch, M. (1973), Psychoanalysis and theory formation. *Annual Psychoanal.*, 1:39–52. New York: Quadrangle.

Beres, D. (1958), Vicissitudes of superego functions and superego precursors in childhood. *The Psychoanalytic Study of the Child*, 13:324–351. New York: International Universities Press.

175

Bergler, E. (1961), *Curable and Incurable Neurotics*. New York: Liveright.

Berliner, B. (1940), Libido and reality in masochism. *Psychoanal. Quart.*, 9:322–333.

_____ (1942), The concept of masochism. *Psychoanal. Rev.*, 29: 386–400.

_____ (1947), On some psychodynamics of masochism. *Psychoanal. Quart.*, 16:459–471.

_____ (1958), The role of object relations in moral masochism. *Psychoanal. Quart.*, 27:38–56.

Bernstein, I. (1957), The role of narcissism in moral masochism. *Psychoanal. Quart.*, 26:358–377.

Blos, P. (1962), *Adolescence*. New York: International Universities Press.

Bradlow, P. (1971), Murder in the initial dream in psychoanalysis. *Bull. Phila. Psychoanal. Assn.*, 21:70–81.

_____ (1973), On reporting an initial dream in psychoanalysis of undisguised sexual activity between family members (abstract). *Bull. Psychoanal. Med.*, 12:18–22.

_____ (1974), The very late first dream reported in psychoanalysis. Paper presented to the American Psychoanalytic Association, Dec. 6.

_____ & Coen, S. J. (1975), The analyst undisguised in the initial dream in psychoanalysis. *Internat. J. Psycho-Anal.*, pp. 415–425.

Brenner, C. (1959), The masochistic character: genesis and treatment. *J. Amer. Psychoanal. Assn.*, 7:197–226.

_____ (1979), Depressive affect, anxiety, and psychic conflict in the phallic-oedipal phase. *Psychoanal. Quart.*, 48:177–197.

Bylinsky, G. (1976), Science is on the trail of the fountain of youth. *Fortune*, 134–140.

Cavenar, J. O., & Nash, J. L. (1976), Dream as a signal for termination. *J. Amer. Psychoanal. Assn.*, 24:425–436.

Cooper, A. (1977), The narcissistic masochistic character. Paper presented to the Association for Psychoanalytic Medicine, May 24.

Dement, W. (1960), Effect of dream deprivation. *Science*, 131: 1705–1707.

De Monchaux, C. (1978), Dreaming and the organizing function of the ego. *Internat. J. Psycho-Anal.*, 59:443–453.

Denkla, W. D. (1975), A time to die. *Life Sciences*, 16:31–44.

———— (1977), Systems analysis of possible mechanisms of mammalian aging. *Mech. Ageing Dev.*, 6:143–152.

Edelson, M. (1972), Language and dreams. *The Psychoanalytic Study of the Child*, 27:203–282. New Haven: Yale University Press.

Eidelberg, L. (1959), Humiliation and masochism. *J. Amer. Psychoanal. Assn.*, 7:274–283.

Eissler, K. (1953), The effect of the structure of the ego on psychoanalytic technique. *J. Amer. Psychoanal. Assn.*, 1:104–143.

Erikson, E. H. (1950), Childhood and Society. New York: Norton.

———— (1954), The dream specimen of psychoanalysis. *J. Amer. Psycho-anal. Assn.*, 2:5–55.

Federn, P. (1928), The ego as subject and object in narcissism. In: *Ego Psychology and the Psychoses*. New York: Basic Books, 1952, pp. 283–322.

Ferenczi, S. (1913), Stages in the development of the sense of reality. In: *Contributions to Psychoanalysis*. New York: Basic Books, 1950, pp. 213–239.

Fine, B. D., Joseph, E. D., & Waldhorn, H. F., eds. (1969), *The Manifest Content of the Dream*. New York: International Universities Press.

Fisher, C. (1965), Psychoanalytic implications of recent research on sleep and dreaming. *J. Amer. Psychiat. Assn.*, 13:197–303.

Fleming, J. (1975), Some observations on object constancy in the psychoanalysis of adults. *J. Amer. Psychoanal. Assn.*, 23:743–759.

Fraiberg, S. (1952), A critical neurosis in a two-and-a-half-year-old girl. *The Psychoanalytic Study of the Child*, 7:173–215. New York: International Universities Press.

Freud, A. (1936), *The Ego and the Mechanisms of Defense*. New York: International Universities Press, 1966.

———— (1958), Adolescence. *The Psychoanalytic Study of the Child*, 13:255–278. New York: International Universities Press.

———— (1968), Acting out. *Internat. J. Psycho-Anal.*, 49:165–170.

Freud, S. (1895), Project for a scientific psychology. In: *The Origins of Psycho-Analysis: Letters to Wilhelm Fliess, Drafts* and Notes: 1887–*1902*, ed. M. Bonaparte, A. Freud, and E. Kris. New York: Basic Books, 1954, pp. 355–445.

———— (1900), The interpretation of dreams. *Standard Edition*, 5. London: Hogarth, 1953.

———— (1905), Three essays on the theory of sexuality. *Standard Edition*, 7:135–245. London: Hogarth, 1953.

———— (1911a), Formulations on the two principles of mental functioning. *Standard Edition*, 12:218–226. London: Hogarth, 1958.

———— (1911b), The handling of dream-interpretation in psychoanalysis. *Standard Edition*, 12:91–96. London: Hogarth, 1958.

———— (1911c), Psycho-analytic notes on an autobiographical account of a case of paranoia. *Standard Edition*, 12:9–82. London: Hogarth, 1958.

———— (1913), The disposition to obsessional neurosis: a contribution to the problem of choice of neurosis. *Standard Edition*, 12:317–326. London: Hogarth, 1958.

———— (1914), On narcissism: an introduction. *Standard Edition*, 14:69–102. London: Hogarth, 1957.

———— (1915), Instincts and their vicissitudes. *Standard Edition*, 14:117–140. London: Hogarth, 1957.

———— (1916a), Introductory lectures on psycho-analysis. *Standard Edition*, 15–16. London: Hogarth, 1963.

———— (1916b), Some character-types met with in psychoanalytic work. *Standard Edition*, 14:311–334. London: Hogarth, 1957.

———— (1917a), Mourning and Melancholia. *Standard Edition*, 14:243–259. London: Hogarth, 1957.

———— (1917b), On transformations of instinct as exemplified in anal eroticism. *Standard Edition*, 17:127–133. London: Hogarth, 1955.

———— (1919), A child is being beaten. *Standard Edition*, 17:179–204. London: Hogarth, 1955.

———— (1920), Beyond the pleasure principle. *Standard Edition*, 18:7–64. London: Hogarth, 1961.

———— (1923a), The ego and the id. *Standard Edition*, 19:12–66. London: Hogarth, 1961.

———— (1923b), Remarks on the theory and practice of dream interpretation. *Standard Edition*, 19:109–121. London: Hogarth, 1961.

_____ (1924), The economic problem of masochism. *Standard Edition,* 19:159–170. London: Hogarth, 1964.

_____ (1926), Inhibitions, symptoms and anxiety. *Standard Edition,* 20:87–156. London: Hogarth, 1964.

_____ (1930), Civilization and its discontents. *Standard Edition,* 21:64–145. London: Hogarth, 1961.

_____ (1932), New introductory lectures on psycho-analysis. *Standard Edition,* 22:5–182. London: Hogarth, 1961.

_____ (1937), Analysis terminable and interminable. *Standard Edition,* 23:216–253. London: Hogarth, 1964.

_____ (1940), An outline of psycho-analysis. *Standard Edition,* 23:144–207. London: Hogarth, 1964.

Gedo, J. E. (1975), Forms of idealization in the analytic transference. *J. Amer. Psychoanal. Assn.,* 23:485–505.

_____ & Goldberg, A. (1973), *Models of the Mind.* Chicago and London: Chicago University Press.

Gero, G. (1936), The construction of depression. *Internat. J. Psycho-Anal.,* 17:423–461.

Glover, E. (1930), Grades of ego differentiation. *Internat. J. Psycho-Anal.,* 11:1–11.

Greenberg, R., & Pearlman, C. (1978), If Freud only knew: a reconsideration of psychoanalytic dream theory. *Internat. Rev. Psycho-Anal.,* 5:71–75.

Hartmann, E. (1967), *The Biology of Dreaming.* Springfield, Ill.: Charles C Thomas.

Hartmann, H. (1939), *Ego Psychology and the Problem of Adaptation.* New York: International Universities Press, 1964.

_____ (1950a), Comments on the psychoanalytic theory of the ego. *The Psychoanalytic Study of the Child,* 5:74–96. New York: International Universities Press.

_____ (1950b), Psychoanalysis and developmental psychology. *The Psychoanalytic Study of the Child,* 5:7–17. New York: International Universities Press.

_____ (1955), Notes on the theory of sublimation. *The Psychoanalytic Study of the Child,* 10:9–29. New York: International Universities Press.

_____, Kris, E., & Loewenstein, R. M. (1946), Comments on the formulation of psychic structure. *The Psychoanalytic*

*Study of the Child,* 2:11–38. New York: International Universities Press.

————— & Loewenstein, R. M. (1962), Notes on the superego. *The Psychoanalytic Study of the Child,* 17:42–81. New York: International Universities Press.

Hegel, G. (1837), *Reason in History.* New York: Liberal Arts Press, 1953.

Heilbrunn, G. (1979), Biological correlates of psychoanalytic concepts. *J. Amer. Psychoanal. Assn.,* 27:597–626.

Isaacs, S. (1929), Privation and guilt. *Internat. J. Psycho-Anal.,* 10:335–347.

Jacobson, E. (1954), The self and the object world. *The Psychoanalytic Study of the Child,* 9:75–126. New York: International Universities Press.

————— (1959), The 'exceptions.' *The Psychoanalytic Study of the Child,* 14:35–54. New York: International Universities Press.

————— (1964), *The Self and the Object World.* New York: International Universities Press.

Jones, E. (1926), The origin and structure of the superego. *Internat. J. Psycho-Anal.,* 7:303–311.

Kernberg, O. (1970), Factors in the psychoanalytic treatment of narcissistic personalities. *J. Amer. Psychoanal. Assn.,* 18:51–85.

————— (1975), *Borderline Conditions and Pathologic Narcissism.* New York: Jason Aronson.

Klein, G. (1976), *Psychoanalytic Theory.* New York: International Universities Press.

Klein, M. (1933), The early development of conscience in the child. In: *Melanie Klein: Contributions to Psychoanalysis.* London: Hogarth, 1948.

————— (1958), On the development of mental functioning. In: *Envy and Gratitude and Other Works, 1946–1963.* New York: Dell, 1977, pp. 236–246.

————— (1959), Our adult world and its roots in infancy: In: *Envy and Gratitude.* Delacorte, 1975, pp. 217–263.

Kohut, H. (1960), Discussion of "Further data and documents in the Schreber case" by William G. Niederland. In: *The Search for the Self* (1978), ed. P. Ornstein. New York: International Universities Press, pp. 305–308.

_____ (1966), Forms and transformations of narcissism. *J. Amer. Psychoanal. Assn.*, 14:243–272.

_____ (1968), The psychoanalytic treatment of narcissistic personality disorders. *The Psychoanalytic Study of the Child*, 23:86–113. New York: International Universities Press.

_____ (1971), *The Analysis of the Self.* New York: International Universities Press.

_____ (1972), Thoughts on narcissism and narcissistic rage. *The Psychoanalytic Study of the Child*, 27:360–400. New Haven: Yale University Press.

_____ (1976), Creativeness, charisma, group psychology: reflections on the self-analysis of Freud. In: *The Search for the Self* (1978), ed. P. Ornstein. New York: International Universities Press, pp. 793–843.

_____ (1977), *The Restoration of the Self.* New York: International Universities Press.

_____ (1979), The two analyses of Mr. Z., *Internat. J. Psycho-Anal.*, 60:3–27.

Kuhn, T. S. (1962), *The Structure of Scientific Revolutions.* Chicago, Ill.: The University of Chicago Press, 1970.

_____ (1970), Logic of discovery or psychology of research: reflections on my critics. In: *Criticism and the Growth of Knowledge*, ed. I. Lakatos and A. Musgrave. London: Cambridge University Press, pp. 1–23, 231–278.

Lampl-de Groot, J. (1962), Ego ideal and superego. *The Psychoanalytic Study of the Child*, 17:94–106. New York: International Universities Press.

Lichtenberg, J. (1978), Discussion of "Psychoanalytic paradigms and their narcissistic investment" by Arnold Rothstein at the Meetings of the American Psychoanalytic Association, Dec., 1978.

Loewald, H. (1960), On the therapeutic action of psychoanalysis. *Internat. J. Psycho-Anal.*, 41:16–33.

_____ (1962), The superego and the ego ideal. *Internat. J. Psycho-Anal.*, 43:264–268.

_____ (1973), Review of *The Analysis of the Self* by Heinz Kohut, *Psychoanal. Quart.*, 42:441–451.

Loewenstein, R. M. (1957), A contribution to the psychoanalytic theory of masochism. *J. Amer. Psychoanal. Assn.*, 5:197–234.

Mahler, M. S. (1971), A study of the separation-individuation process and its possible application to borderline phenomena. *The Psychoanalytic Study of the Child*, 26:403–424. New York: Quadrangle.

———— (1972), On the three subphases of the separation-individuation process. *Internat. J. Psycho-Anal.*, 53:333–338.

———— Pine, F., & Bergman, A. (1975), *The Psychological Birth of the Human Infant*. New York: Basic Books.

Mehlman, R. D. (1976), Transference mobilization, transference resolution and the narcissistic alliance. Paper presented to the Boston Psychoanalytic Society and Institute, Feb. 25.

Meiss, M. (1952), The oedipal problems of a fatherless child. *The Psychoanalytic Study of the Child*, 7:216–229. New York: International Universities Press.

Meissner, W. W. (1981), *Internalization in Psychoanalysis*. New York: International Universities Press.

Menaker, E. (1953), Masochism: a defensive reaction of the ego. *Psychoanal. Quart.*, 22:205–220.

Modell, A. (1976), "The holding environment" and the therapeutic action of psychoanalysis. *J. Amer. Psychoanal. Assn.*, 24: 285–307.

Nagera, H. (1969), Basic psychoanalytic concepts on the theory of dreams. *Hampstead Clinic Psycho-Analytic Library*, Vol. I. New York: Basic Books.

Niederland, W. (1959), The "miracled-up" world of Schreber's childhood. *The Psychoanalytic Study of the Child*, 14:383–413. New York: International Universities Press.

Nunberg, H. (1932), *Principles of Psychoanalysis: Their Application to the Neuroses*. New York: International Universities Press, 1955.

Olinick, S. (1964), The negative therapeutic reaction. *Internat. J. Psycho-Anal.*, 45:540–548.

Oremland, J. (1973), A specific dream during the termination phase of successful psychoanalysis. *J. Amer. Psychoanal. Assn.*, 21:285–302.

Ornstein, P. (1978), The evaluation of Heinz Kohut's psychoanalytic psychology of the self. In: *The Search for the Self*. New York: International Universities Press, pp. 1–106.

Parkin, A. (1980), On masochistic enthrallment: a contribution to the study of moral masochism. *Internat. J. Psycho-Anal.*, 61:307–314.

Peterfreund, E. (1971), *Information, Systems and Psychoanalysis.* New York: International Universities Press.

Piers, G., & Singer, M. (1953), *Shame and Guilt.* Springfield, Ill.: Charles C Thomas.

Polumbo, S. R. (1976), The dream and the memory cycle. *Internat. Rev. Psycho-Anal.*, 3:65–83.

Rangell, L. (1956), The dream in the practice of psychoanalysis. *J. Amer. Psychoanal. Assn.*, 4:122–137.

Rappaport, D. (1959), A historical survey of psychoanalytic ego psychology. In: *Identity and the Life Cycle,* ed. E. H. Erikson. New York: International Universities Press.

Reich, A. (1953), Narcissistic object choice in women. *J. Amer. Psychoanal. Assn.*, 1:22–44.

_____ (1954), Early identifications as archaic elements in the superego. *J. Amer. Psychoanal. Assn.*, 2:218–238.

_____ (1960), Pathologic forms of self-esteem regulation. *The Psychoanalytic Study of the Child,* 15:215–231. New York: International Universities Press.

Reich, W. (1933), *Character Analysis.* New York: Noonday.

Rosenblum, L., & Harlow, H. (1963), Approach-avoidance conflict in the mother-surrogate situation, *Psychol. Reports,* 12:83–85.

Rosenfeld, H. (1962), The superego and the ego-ideal. *Internat. J. Psycho-Anal.*, 43:258–263.

Rothstein, A. (1979a), An exploration of the diagnostic term narcissistic personality disorder. *J. Amer. Psychoanal. Assn.*, 27:893–912.

_____ (1979b), Oedipal conflicts in narcissistic personality disorders, *Internat. J. Psycho-Anal.*, 60:189–199.

_____ (1980a), *The Narcissistic Pursuit of Perfection.* New York: International Universities Press.

_____ (1980b), Psychoanalytic paradigms and their narcissistic investment. *J. Amer. Psychoanal. Assn.*, 28:385–395.

_____ (1980c), Toward a critique of the psychology of the self. *Psychoanal. Quart.*, 49:423–455.

_____ (1982), The implications of early psychopathology for the analyzability of narcissistic personality disorders. *Internat. J. Psycho-Anal.*, 63:177–188.

Sacks, R. L., & Miller, W. (1975), Masochism, clinical and theoretical overview. *Psychiatry,* 38:244–257.

Sander, L. (1962), Issues in early mother-child interaction. *J. Amer. Acad. of Child Psych.,* 1:141–166.

Sandler, J. (1960), On the concept of superego. *The Psychoanalytic Study of the Child,* 15:128–162. New York: International Universities Press.

_____ & Rosenblatt, B. (1962), The concept of the representational world. *The Psychoanalytic Study of the Child,* 17:128–145. New York: International Universities Press.

Schafer, R. (1960), The loving and beloved superego in Freud's structural theory. *The Psychoanalytic Study of the Child,* 15:163–168. New York: International Universities Press.

_____ (1968), *Aspects of Internalization.* New York: International Universities Press.

_____ (1976), *A New Language for Psychoanalysis.* New Haven: Yale University Press.

Schucker, E. (1979), Psychodynamics and treatment of sexual assault victims. *J. Amer. Acad. Psychoanal.,* 7:553–573.

Segal, N. (1969), Repetition compulsion, acting-out, and identification with the doer. *J. Amer. Psychoanal. Assn.,* 17:474–488.

Socarides, C. W. (1958), The function of moral masochism: with special reference to the defense process. *Internat. J. Psycho-Anal.,* 39:587–597.

Spanjaard, J. (1969), The manifest content and its significance for the interpretation of dreams. *Internat. J. Psycho-Anal.,* 50:221–235.

Stein, M. (1956), Report of the panel on the problem of masochism in the theory and technique of psychoanalysis. *J. Amer. Psychoanal. Assn.,* 4:526–538.

_____ (1973), Acting out as a character trait. *The Psychoanalytic Study of the Child,* 28:347–364. New Haven: Yale University Press.

_____ (1979), Book review of Kohut's "Restoration of the Self." *J. Amer. Psychoanal. Assn.,* 27:665–680.

Stevenson, R. L. (1886), *Dr. Jekyll & Mr. Hyde.* New York: Bantam, 1967.

Stewart, W. A. (1969), Comments on the manifest content of certain types of unusual dreams. In: *The Manifest Content of the*

*Dream,* ed. B. D. Fine, et al. New York: International Universities Press, pp. 81–91.

Stone, L. (1954), The widening scope of psychoanalysis. *J. Amer. Psychoanal. Assn.,* 2:567–594.

Strachey, R. (1934), The nature of the therapeutic action of psycho-analysis. *Internat. J. Psycho-Anal.,* 15:127–159.

Sulloway, F. J. (1979), *Freud, Biologist of the Mind.* New York: Basic Books.

Tolstoy, L. (1878), *Anna Karenina,* New York: Random House, 1965.

Valenstein, A. S. (1973), On attachments to painful feelings and the negative therapeutic reaction. *The Psychoanalytic Study of the Child,* 28:365–392. New York: Yale University Press.

Waelder, R. (1930), The principle of multiple function: observations on over-determination. *Psychoanal. Quart.,* 5:45–62.

_____ (1960), *Basic Theory of Psychoanalysis.* New York: International Universities Press.

Weil, A. P. (1970), The basic core. *The Psychoanalytic Study of the Child.,* 25:442–460. New York: International Universities Press.

Weissman, P. (1954), Ego and superego in obsessional character and neurosis. *Psychoanal. Quart.,* 23:529–543.

Winnicott, D. W. (1960), The theory of the parent-infant relationship. In: *The Maturational Processes and the Facilitating Environment.* New York: International Universities Press, 1965, pp. 37–55.

Wolfenstein, M. (1966), How is mourning possible? *The Psychoanalytic Study of the Child,* 21:93–123. New York: International Universities Press.

_____ (1969), Loss, rage, repetition. *The Psychoanalytic Study of the Child,* 24:432–446. New York: International Universities Press.

# Index

187